OUR WORLD, OUR STORIES

Dave Rear

photographs by
iStockphoto
Shutterstock

音声ファイルのダウンロード／ストリーミング

CDマーク表示がある箇所は、音声を弊社HPより無料でダウンロード／ストリーミングすることができます。下記URLの書籍詳細ページに音声ダウンロードアイコンがございますのでそちらから自習用音声としてご活用ください。

https://seibido.co.jp/ad722

Our World, Our Stories

Copyright © 2025 by Dave Rear

All rights reserved for Japan.
No part of this book may be reproduced in any form
without permission from Seibido Co., Ltd.

To Teachers and Students

Welcome to *Our World, Our Stories*. This textbook delves into the fascinating subjects that shape our contemporary landscape. From groundbreaking scientific discoveries to evolving cultural trends and the challenges of today's global societies, it covers an array of topics designed to spark curiosity and encourage critical thinking. Each unit aims to provoke thoughtful discussions and equip students with a broader understanding of the world around them.

The book is divided into four sections of five units each. We begin with Economy and Work, where we learn about companies that have banned meetings, the rise of the four-day work week, and the secrets of Red Bull marketing. Then we move onto Humans and Society. What are the advantages and disadvantages of tourism? Is it better to know what will happen or to be uncertain? What's it like to walk around the world? In the third section, we turn to Media and Entertainment. We ask whether video games can be good for us, why we can't always trust newspapers, and how Disney managed to take over the world. In the final section, Science and Technology, we delve into topics as diverse as the spooky science of ghosts, the miracle of the James Webb Space Telescope, and the fledgling technology of living robots. Whatever your particular interest, you're sure to learn something new.

To engage the students and extend their language skills, the textbook contains a variety of activities to complete in and out of class. Each unit begins with a short discussion to introduce the major theme. Then there are a pair of comprehension exercises to test the students' understanding of the main reading. This is followed by a vocabulary exercise to cover essential words and then a short summary and listening. The unit ends with a longer discussion and writing activity in which students express their opinions about the topic.

I hope you enjoy teaching and studying with the book. Best of luck!

Dave Rear

Table of Contents

Section I: Economy and Work　　経済と仕事

Unit 1　**Pressure to Please: Why can't we say no?**
人を喜ばせるプレッシャー：ノーと言えないのはなぜか...06

Unit 2　**No Time to Waste: Should we ban meetings?**
時間を無駄にしない：企業は会議を禁止するべきか...12

Unit 3　**Marketing Genius: How did Red Bull achieve its success?**
マーケティングの天才：レッドブル社はいかにして成功を収めたのか...................19

Unit 4　**Trains, Planes, and Automobiles: What is a Super Commuter?**
電車，飛行機，車：超長距離通勤とは何か...25

Unit 5　**Long Weekends: Should we work four days a week?**
長い週末：週休三日制を導入するべきか...32

Section II: Humans and Society　　人間と社会

Unit 6　**Tourism: Is it a blessing or a curse?**
観光：それは祝福なのか，それとも災いか...39

Unit 7　**Agony of Uncertainty: Is it better to know what will happen?**
不確実性の苦しみ：将来の出来事を予期すべきか...46

Unit 8　**A Long Way to Go: What's it like to walk around the world?**
長い道のり：人はなぜ世界を歩くのか...53

Unit 9　**Lost Cities: Are they myth or reality?**
失われた都市：それは神話か，現実か...59

Unit 10　**An Ordinary Hero: How did one man stop World War III?**
ヒーローになった普通の男：どのように第三次世界大戦を止めたのか.............66

Section III: Media and Entertainment　メディアとエンターテインメント

Unit 11　**Left or Right: What is bias in the media?**
左か右か：マスコミの偏向報道とは何か 73

Unit 12　**Gaming to Success: Can video games be good for us?**
ゲームで成功する：テレビゲームは私たちのためになるのか 80

Unit 13　**Digital Town Square: Why is Twitter always in the news?**
自由な会話の場：なぜツイッターは話題になるのか 87

Unit 14　**For Love Not Money: Is there a dark side to working in Hollywood?**
お金ではなく愛のために：ハリウッドで働く影の側面とは 94

Unit 15　**Entertainment Empire: How did Disney take over the world?**
エンターテイメントの帝国：ディズニーはどのように世界を席巻したのか 101

Section IV: Science and Technology　科学と技術

Unit 16　**Spooky Science: Are ghosts real?**
不気味な科学：幽霊は実在するのか 108

Unit 17　**Believing a Lie: Can we plant memories in the brain?**
記憶の書き換え：脳に記憶を植え付けることはできるのか 114

Unit 18　**Cell Magic: Can we make a living robot?**
細胞のマジック：生きたロボットは作れるか 121

Unit 19　**Looking into the Past: What is the James Webb Space Telescope?**
過去に目を向ける：ジェームス・ウェッブ宇宙望遠鏡とは何か 128

Unit 20　**New Solution: Can we turn carbon dioxide into stone?**
新しいソリューション：二酸化炭素を石に変えることはできるか 135

UNIT 1

Pressure to Please

Why can't we say no?

Introduction

Have you ever been asked to do something you didn't want to do, but, instead of refusing, found yourself saying yes? If so, you're not alone. Research has shown that it is very difficult for human beings to say no, even if we are asked to do something unethical. Why is this?

Activate Your Thinking

Think about the following questions and share your ideas with your classmates.

1. Have you ever said yes to something you didn't want to do?
   _____
   _____

2. Why do you think it is hard for people to say no to requests?
   _____
   _____

UNIT 1 | **Pressure to Please**

Reading

🔊 1-03~10

Read the passage and check that you understand the underlined words.

🔊 1-03

When Takashi's boss at his fast-food restaurant asked him to work an extra shift to cover an absent co-worker, Takashi knew he should say no. He had end-of-term exams coming up at his university and, while the extra money from his part-time job was always welcome, his studies were his main priority. He hesitated before answering, hoping his pained expression would be enough for his boss to understand his feelings. But, at the same time, he also knew his boss wouldn't have asked him unless it was necessary. After all, the restaurant had to stay open no matter how short-staffed it was. Slowly, he found himself nodding his head. "Sure, just one extra shift would be okay, I guess," he replied. His boss's grateful smile told him how much his sacrifice meant.

🔊 1-04

Many of us have been in Takashi's situation, whether it is being asked to work an extra shift or carry out some other task we aren't happy about doing. It is that feeling of wanting to say no but somehow finding ourselves agreeing to it instead. Why do we find it so difficult to refuse a request? For the past 15 years, a social psychologist at Cornell University in the United States named Vanessa Bohns has been trying to find out.

🔊 1-05

Her work builds on an experiment carried out in the 1970s by Ellen Langer at Harvard University. In Langer's study, participants were told to go to the university library and attempt to cut in line for the photocopier. Langer wanted to know how many people would allow someone to go in front of them. Her results were interesting. If the participant gave a reason for cutting in line, over 94 percent of people allowed them to go ahead, compared to 60 percent when the participant offered no excuse at all. The reason they gave, however, didn't have to be a good one. Even if the participant simply said they "needed to make some copies," which isn't an excuse at all, people agreed to let them do it. The experiment suggested that we are willing to agree to a request with only the smallest amount of encouragement.

🔊 1-06

Bohns's own research confirmed Langer's results. In one experiment, she had participants approach strangers and ask them to complete a survey. The participants predicted they would have to ask at least four people to get a response, but in fact it was closer to two. In another study, they asked a stranger to walk them to a nearby gym, explaining they couldn't find it. To their surprise, they found that one in two people agreed to help, even though it meant walking away from their original route.

CD 1-07

We might interpret these results positively as a sign of basic human kindness. But in some of Bohns's other studies, a darker side was seen. Participants in one study were told to approach strangers with the following request: "Hi, I'm trying to play a prank on someone, but they know my handwriting. Will you write the word 'pickle' on the page of this library book?" Bohns did not expect anyone to agree to vandalize the book, but despite raising some objections, more than half the people agreed to do it. This finding was repeated in other studies when, for example, strangers were asked to falsify academic documents.

CD 1-08

Bohns drew two conclusions from her work. First, people are surprisingly willing to agree to a request even if it is clearly an unethical act; and second, we tend to underestimate our power to persuade other people to do what we want. We don't think about their fear of embarrassment and assume they will be <u>courageous</u> enough to refuse. In reality, however, human beings are a social <u>species</u>, and they naturally try to avoid things that might damage their relationships with others. By refusing a request, we risk that the other person will feel humiliated, or, as they say in psychology, "lose face," and so we try hard to stop that from happening. And in Bohns's studies, remember, the participants were all of equal status. Refusing a request that comes from someone higher in the hierarchy – a boss or teacher, for example – is even harder.

CD 1-09

The lesson here is not necessarily that we should all be braver to say no; it is that we have to be careful how we request things of others. We need to give people room to reject things they don't want to do. It is easier, for example, to say no over email than face to face or over the phone, so consider approaching people in writing first. Or, if you feel it is more polite to talk face to face, ask for their response later rather than <u>straightaway</u>. "You can give the person a little more space to gather their thoughts," advises Bohns.

UNIT 1 | Pressure to Please

1-10

Would Takashi have refused his boss's request if it had been expressed in a different way? We might never know, but getting people to do things they feel uncomfortable with is not a good way to build a positive, long-term relationship. Our power to influence people is much stronger than we assume.

65

NOTES

pained expression 苦痛にゆがんだ表情　　**social psychologist** 社会心理学者　　**cut in line** 順番を抜かす，列に割り込む　　**interpret** 解釈する　　**play a prank** いたずらをする　　**vandalize** 落書きする　　**raise an objection** 異議を唱える　　**falsify** 偽造する　　**unethical** 非倫理的　　**underestimate** 過少評価する　　**feel humiliated** 屈辱を感じる　　**lose face** 面目を失う　　**hierarchy** ヒエラルキー，段階的組織

Reading Comprehension

Decide if each sentence is true or false.

1. [T / F]　Takashi agreed to work an extra shift even though he was unhappy about it.

2. [T / F]　People agree with requests only if a good reason is given.

3. [T / F]　Bohns was surprised how many people agreed to damage the library book.

4. [T / F]　People tend to underestimate how difficult it is to refuse a request.

5. [T / F]　It should be considered rude to send a request by email.

Finding Details

Write down the answer to each question.

1. What were participants in Ellen Langer's study told to do in the university library?

   _____

2. Around what percentage of people agreed to show participants to the gym?

   _____

3. What term in psychology is used to describe a feeling of humiliation?

   _____

9

Extend Your Vocabulary

Choose the correct word from the list to complete each sentence.

| priority | hesitate | courageous | species | straightaway |

1. The student got to work on her project _____.

2. My _____ is to complete this assignment before anything else.

3. Please don't _____ to contact me if you have any questions.

4. Saving that child from the river was a really _____ act.

5. The researchers discovered a new _____ of insect in the rainforest.

Summary

CD 1-11

Listen to the audio and fill in the spaces.

Have you ever agreed to a (1) _____ even though you didn't really want to? If so, you are not alone. Through her studies, social psychologist Vanessa Bohns has shown that people do not like to (2) _____ to do things. In one study, for example, 94 percent of people allowed someone to cut in line for the (3) _____ even if the excuse given was inappropriate. In another, over half agreed to vandalize a library book, although it was clearly an unethical act. Bohns says human beings try hard to make sure the other person doesn't lose face, and this makes them (4) _____ to agree to things they do not really want to do. When we make a request, therefore, we should try to (5) _____ it in such a way that the other person has room to say no.

UNIT 1 | Pressure to Please

Expressing Your Opinion

→ Discussion

What do you think about the following statement? Think of two reasons for your opinion and share them with your classmates. Try to add details or examples and continue your conversation for as long as you can.

People in Japan care too much about how they are viewed by others.

5. Strongly Agree   4. Agree   3. Neither agree nor disagree
2. Disagree   1. Strongly disagree

Reason 1: _____

_____

_____

Reason 2: _____

_____

_____

→ Paragraph Writing

Finish this short paragraph about the opinion above. Give details or examples for your reasons.

I think / don't think that people in Japan care too much about how they are

viewed by others. First, _____

_____

_____

_____

_____

_____

11

UNIT 2

No Time to Waste

Should we ban meetings?

Introduction

Nobody really enjoys meetings, and yet they are a large part of the modern workplace. Some companies, however, have taken the step of banning meetings, viewing them as a waste of their employees' time. What are the advantages and disadvantages of doing so?

Activate Your Thinking

Think about the following questions and share your ideas with your classmates.

1. Have you ever been in a long meeting? What was it about and how long did it last? _____

   _____

2. Do you think people have too many meetings in Japan?

   _____

   _____

12

UNIT 2 | No Time to Waste

Reading

CD 1-13~20

Read the passage and check that you understand the underlined words.

CD 1-13

Peter Drucker, the famous management consultant, once wrote: "Meetings are a symptom of bad organization. The fewer meetings the better." It's fair to say that Drucker was not the only person who disliked meetings. In fact, it would be hard to find someone who woke up in the morning and thought: "Hey, you know what I'd like to do today? Have a lot of meetings!" But even though few people seem to enjoy them, meetings have become a fundamental aspect of the modern workplace. Research shows that executives spend almost 23 hours a week in them on average, while for workers further down the hierarchy, it is rare to get through a week without at least two or three.

CD 1-14

With the rise in remote working during the coronavirus pandemic, you might have thought that meetings would have declined in number. But far from it. Analysis by Harvard Business School showed that although meetings were on average 12 percent shorter than before the pandemic, people were attending 13 percent more of them. Formal Zoom sessions seem to have replaced casual chats at the desk.

CD 1-15

So, why do we have so many? What are the advantages of spending so much of our working day in discussion with colleagues? For Steven Rogelberg, a business professor at the University of North Carolina, meetings are a fundamental part of human nature. Humans are social animals for whom working together in groups comes instinctively. "We've gathered since caveman days," he explains. "Meetings are a manifestation of human tendencies." By discussing problems together, we can reach creative solutions that might be out of reach to individuals working alone. For members of a team working on a project, meetings can be a way to share information, brainstorm ideas, clarify goals, and ensure everyone is moving in the same direction. They also provide accountability. It is harder to avoid completing tasks or taking responsibility if you know you have to provide a regular, face-to-face update on your progress.

13

🎧 1-16

Meetings do, however, come with significant downsides. The largest of these is time. It is not only the meeting itself that takes time, but also the need to prepare for it beforehand and reflect on it afterwards. There is a cost on the physical and mental energy of participants, which can have a negative effect on their productivity. Moreover, for every meeting that is effective for generating new ideas, there are several more that achieve almost nothing. For Professor Rogelberg, it is not meetings themselves that are the problem but bad meetings, ones that have no clear focus or goal. "We're still a mess at them and have a long way to go," he says. "There are so many issues: a lack of meaningful training, a lack of feedback on how well they're run, and not enough facilitation from leaders to ensure everyone is contributing." A survey conducted by the consulting firm Korn Ferry reported that 34 percent of employees feel they waste up to five hours per week on pointless gatherings.

🎧 1-17

So, what would happen if we decided to just not have meetings at all? Would that improve the productivity of a firm? Perhaps unsurprisingly, there are companies that have banned meetings altogether, believing them to be a waste of their employees' time. Digital publisher TheSoul Publishing is one of them. A global company with over 2,000 employees, it produces content for YouTube, TikTok and other social media sites, creating more than 1,500 videos each month. Its workers, 80 percent of whom work remotely, are banned from holding meetings, either in-person or online. If they want to speak to a manager, they must book a one-on-one call with at least 24 hours' notice under exceptional circumstances only. "It has to be a very specific goal, not a general brainstorm you can do with other tools," explains content creator Victor Potrel. These other tools include messaging services like Slack but not old-fashioned email. Emails, too, are banned within the company.

🎧 1-18

For Victor Potrel, the absence of meetings has been beneficial, allowing him to concentrate on the creative work where he can most add value to the firm. Socially, he doesn't miss the opportunity to chat with colleagues. He can share his interests via Slack or meet outside of work.

🎧 1-19

But a no-meetings policy doesn't work everywhere. Companies like TheSoul Publishing were set up with the rule already established. It is much harder to ban meetings in an environment where they are the norm. Professor

UNIT 2 | No Time to Waste

Rogelberg knows firms that have tried introducing particular days where meetings are not permitted, but the result has been a sharp increase in emails, with a quick question-and-answer session replaced by a long morning of "email ping pong."

65

1-20

Rogelberg recommends reform rather than removal: "The goal isn't to eliminate meetings, it's to eliminate the bad ones." He suggests limiting the size and length of meetings to force participants to reach a conclusion quickly. He also thinks managers should receive training to learn how to conduct a meeting successfully. "You need to make them effective," he concludes. "Just banning them on an afternoon isn't enough."

70

NOTES

symptom 徴候 **instinctively** 本能的に **caveman days** 原始時代［原始時代に人々が洞窟に住んでいたことから，スラング表現として使われるようになった］ **manifestation** 現れ **tendencies** 傾向 **out of reach** 手が届かない **clarify** 明確にする **accountability** 責任 **downside** デメリット **productivity** 生産性 **be a mess at** 〜が苦手，に失敗する **facilitation** ファシリテーション，円滑化 **24 hours' notice** 24 時間以上前に **beneficial** 良い，功を奏する［benefit の形容詞］ **the norm** 当たり前なこと，常識

Reading Comprehension

Decide if each sentence is true or false.

1. [T / F] Peter Drucker believed that organizations should not have so many meetings.

2. [T / F] The coronavirus pandemic reduced the length but not the number of meetings.

3. [T / F] Steven Rogelberg thinks that holding meetings comes naturally to humans.

4. [T / F] Rogelberg says it is a good idea for companies to ban meetings.

5. [T / F] At TheSoul Publishing, employees can never speak with a manager.

Finding Details

Write down the answer to each question.

1. Why did people attend more meetings during the coronavirus pandemic, according to the article?

_____

2. How do workers at TheSoul Publishing usually communicate with each other?

_____

3. When firms suddenly introduce no-meeting days, what tends to increase as a result?

_____

Extend Your Vocabulary

Choose the correct word from the list to complete each sentence.

fundamental	ensure	effective	survey	eliminate

1. I was asked to cooperate in a _____ over the telephone.

2. We must _____ that we complete the project on time.

3. I don't believe it will be a very _____ strategy.

4. It is impossible to _____ all mistakes from our work.

5. The professor's research is _____ to our understanding of the subject.

UNIT 2 | No Time to Waste

Summary

 1-21

Listen to the audio and fill in the spaces.

Even though few people seem to enjoy them, meetings are a feature of the modern (1) _____. For business professor Steven Rogelberg, it is not surprising that workers within (2) _____ tend to gather to exchange opinions and ideas, since communicating with each other in groups is a fundamental part of being human. He says the problem is not meetings themselves but the fact we (3) _____ so much time in bad ones. Aiming to increase productivity, some companies have taken the step of (4) _____ meetings completely. TheSoul Publishing, an online media company, is one of them. It encourages its (5) _____ to communicate via messaging services rather than face to face. Rogelberg says this approach might work for some organizations but not others. For him, rather than eliminating meetings, we should focus on making them more effective.

Expressing Your Opinion

→ Discussion

What do you think about the following statement? Think of two reasons for your opinion and share them with your classmates. Try to add details or examples and continue your conversation for as long as you can.

Companies should have at least one day a week when meetings are banned.

5. Strongly Agree   4. Agree   3. Neither agree nor disagree

2. Disagree   1. Strongly disagree

Reason 1: _____

_____

_____

Reason 2: _____

_____

_____

→ Paragraph Writing

Finish this short paragraph about the opinion above. Give details or examples for your reasons.

I think / don't think that companies should ban meetings for at least one day a

week. First, _____

_____

_____

_____

_____

_____

UNIT 3

Marketing Genius

How did Red Bull achieve its success?

Introduction

You are surely familiar with the Red Bull energy drink, which can be found in stores all over Japan. But did you know that Red Bull neither invented nor manufactures the drink? The story of the third most valuable soft drink brand in the world is one of marketing. How did they achieve their success?

Activate Your Thinking

Think about the following questions and share your ideas with your classmates.

1. Do you like energy drinks? Which brand do you usually drink?

   _____

   _____

2. What image does Red Bull bring to your mind?

   _____

   _____

Reading 🎧 1-23〜29

Read the passage and check that you understand the underlined words.

🎧 1-23

Here are two facts about Red Bull you might not know. First, it is not a soft drink company. It doesn't <u>manufacture</u> the product it so successfully sells. In fact, it didn't even invent the drink. Second, the famous logo it employs of two bulls about to fight each other does not come from the aggressive animal we are familiar with from dairy farms. It is actually a relatively rare type of bison from Southeast Asia known as a *gaur*. The original name of Red Bull was Krating Daeng, meaning "red gaur."

🎧 1-24

So, how did a drink company that is not a drink company come to sell a product it didn't invent using a name it didn't really come up with? And how did it do it with such success that it is now the third most <u>valuable</u> soft drink brand in the world behind Coca Cola and Pepsi? To answer these questions, we have to travel back to Thailand in 1982, when an Austrian toothpaste executive held a meeting with a local businessman named Chaleo Yoovidhya. Yoovidhya was a pharmacist, the owner of T. C. Pharmaceutical, and one of his products was a cheap energy drink called Krating Daeng, rather like the Japanese brand Lipovitan, which was popular with laborers and truck drivers. The Austrian, Dietrich Mateschitz, was suffering from jet lag, and Yoovidhya offered him a bottle to help him wake up. As it happened, however, the drink did more than cure the executive's jet lag; it inspired him to offer the Thai entrepreneur a deal.

🎧 1-25

Two years later, the company Red Bull GmbH was born. Mateschitz and Yoovidhya both <u>invested</u> $500,000 of their own money and took a 49 percent share in the company each, giving the remaining 2 percent to Yoovidhya's son. The pair worked hard to make the Thai drink more attractive to Western tastes, carbonating it to make it fizzy and making it less sweet. Choosing to sell it in the slim cans familiar to consumers today, they launched the product in Austria in 1987.

🎧 1-26

From the beginning, Mateschitz's focus was on how to market the new drink in the incredibly crowded and competitive soft drink industry. While Krating

UNIT 3 | **Marketing Genius**

Daeng was popular with working-class men, Red Bull positioned itself as a trendy, upmarket product, and was priced accordingly. The market for energy drinks didn't exist in Europe or the United States, so Mateschitz set out to create one from scratch, aiming at a demographic of sporty 18- to 34-year-old males. He began by traveling to sports events and handing out free samples of the drink, along with other kinds of merchandise covered in Red Bull logos. This was very different from a traditional marketing approach, which relied on print and television advertisements.

🎧 1-27

The free samples helped Red Bull to spread its popularity through word-of-mouth. But what really helped it to take off was sponsoring sports events, particularly the kind of extreme sports popular with its target demographic. The first event it gave its name to was the Dolomitenmann, otherwise known as "the toughest team contest under the sun." Consisting of mountain running, paragliding, mountain biking, and wildwater kayaking, it drew exactly the hardcore audience Red Bull was hoping to attract to its brand. Another well-known event was the Space Jump made by Austrian skydiver Felix Baumgartner in 2012 as part of the Red Bull Stratos project. Jumping from a record height of 39 kilometers inside the Earth's stratosphere, the adventurer reached a top speed of 1,357 kilometers per hour on his descent before he landed safely in New Mexico in the U.S. The stunt attracted 8 million viewers to the live stream and many more afterwards on Facebook, YouTube, Twitter, and other social media sites. It is considered one of the most successful marketing achievements of all time, perfectly suiting the energy drink's slogan of "Red Bull gives you wings."

🎧 1-28

Nowadays, Red Bull has gone further than simply sponsoring events. Using the profits gained from selling over 11 billion cans per year in 167 countries, it has bought or created teams in motor racing, soccer, ice hockey, and esports. It currently owns seven soccer teams in Austria, Germany, Brazil, Ghana, and the United States, most famously RB Leipzig, which it managed to bring up from the German fifth division all the way to the first division, the Bundesliga, in just seven seasons. Of all its sports ownerships, it is the company's Formula 1 team that generates the most publicity for its brand. One of the most successful teams in the whole of motor racing, it has won six championships at the time of writing, including in 2021, 2022, and 2023 under its lead driver Max Verstappen.

1-29

The story of Red Bull shows what can be done with a mixture of marketing expertise and a willingness to take risks. Despite its global presence, Red Bull and its sister-drink, Krating Daeng, are still manufactured by T. C. Pharmaceutical from its headquarters in Bangkok, Thailand. Although Dietrich Mateschitz passed away in 2022, the partnership he created with Thai businessman Chaleo Yoovidhya lives on.

NOTES

laborer 労働者　　**jet lag** 時差ボケ　　**entrepreneur** 起業家　　**carbonate** 発泡させる　　**fizzy** 炭酸　　**upmarket** 高級な　　**from scratch** 一から　　**demographic** 層, 人口　　**merchandise** グッズ, 商品　　**word-of-mouth** クチコミ　　**hardcore** 筋金入り　　**stratosphere** 成層圏　　**pass away** 亡くなる

Reading Comprehension

Decide if each sentence is true or false.

1. [T / F]　Red Bull was born through a meeting between a toothpaste executive and a pharmacist.

2. [T / F]　Red Bull is jointly owned by an Austrian and a Thai company.

3. [T / F]　Krating Daeng and Red Bull both aim at a similar demographic.

4. [T / F]　Felix Baumgartner made the highest jump ever by a human.

5. [T / F]　RB Leipzig is a rare example of a project that did not bring success to Red Bull.

Finding Details

Write down the answer to each question.

1. Why did Chaleo Yoovidhya offer his meeting partner a drink of Krating Daeng?

_____

2. How did the two owners of Red Bull alter the taste of Krating Daeng?

_____

3. What sports team owned by Red Bull gives the firm the most publicity?

_____

UNIT 3 | Marketing Genius

Extend Your Vocabulary

Choose the correct word from the list to complete each sentence.

| manufacture | valuable | invest | sample | publicity |

1. The bank decided to _____ money in a new company.

2. The _____ we will get from sponsoring the event will make up for its cost.

3. The antique watch was so _____ that the man kept it in a safe.

4. This is just a small _____ of the product we are hoping to sell.

5. We will _____ the car in a factory we are building in Taiwan.

Summary

1-30

Listen to the audio and fill in the spaces.

It might surprise you to hear that Red Bull does not manufacture the product it sells and nor did it (1) _____ it. The brand came about when an Austrian executive named Dietrich Mateschitz had a meeting with a Thai (2) _____ called Chaleo Yoovidhya and tried the Thai entrepreneur's energy drink to cure his jet lag. Forming a partnership, the two men made changes to the drink to suit Western tastes and then began to sell it in Austria under the name Red Bull. Since the energy drink market did not (3) _____ in Europe, Mateschitz set out to create one from scratch by handing out free samples of the product at sports events. Aiming at a market of young, sporty men, Red Bull began (4) _____ competitions and then creating events itself, such as the Space Jump made by Austrian skydiver Felix Baumgartner in 2012. Now Red Bull is the third most valuable soft drink brand in the world (5) _____ Coca Cola and Pepsi.

23

Expressing Your Opinion

→ Discussion

What do you think about the following statement? Think of two reasons for your opinion and share them with your classmates. Try to add details or examples and continue your conversation for as long as you can.

Marketing is the most important part of a company.

5. Strongly Agree   4. Agree   3. Neither agree nor disagree
2. Disagree   1. Strongly disagree

Reason 1: _____

_____

_____

Reason 2: _____

_____

_____

→ Paragraph Writing

Finish this short paragraph about the opinion above. Give details or examples for your reasons.

I think / don't think that marketing is the most important part of a company.

First, _____

_____

_____

_____

_____

_____

UNIT 4

Trains, Planes, and Automobiles

What is a super commuter?

Introduction

When we think of commuting, most people imagine traveling into the city center on a crowded train. But for some people, this is only the final leg of their journey to work. Before that, they have driven to the airport, passed through security, and caught a plane. Welcome to the world of the super commuter.

Activate Your Thinking

Think about the following questions and share your ideas with your classmates.

1. How long is your commute to school? What do you do to pass the time?

   _____
   _____

2. What is the longest commute you would be willing to do for work?

   _____
   _____

Reading

🎧 1-32~38

Read the passage and check that you understand the underlined words.

🎧 1-32

Tokyoites might complain about their morning commute from the suburbs on crowded trains. But spare a thought for David Bearce, whose journey to work takes him from his family home in Minneapolis all the way to central New York, some 1,600 kilometers away. To reach his office, he first drives by car to Minneapolis Airport, takes a two-and-a-half-hour flight to New York, followed by a 35-minute train into Manhattan, and finally a 10-minute walk through the crowded city streets. Door to door, it takes him approximately five hours.

🎧 1-33

David Bearce is the husband of writer Megan Bearce, author, appropriately enough, of the book *Super Commuter Couples: Staying Together When a Job Keeps You Apart*. His massive commute came about when he was offered a dream job in America's largest city just six months after buying a house in Minneapolis. Rather than trying to sell their spacious new home, they decided to give super commuting a try. Four years later, they are still doing it. David travels to New York on Monday morning and stays there for two nights, returning to Minneapolis on Wednesday evening. On Thursday and Friday, he is able to work remotely. The travel and accommodation expenses are not inconsiderable, but they are compensated for by the lower living costs in Minneapolis and the higher New York salary. "It's actually been really great," says Megan, though she advises would-be commuters to "weigh what it is costing you financially and emotionally."

🎧 1-34

David Bearce is an extreme example, but super commuting is a surprisingly common phenomenon around the world, depending on exactly how the term is defined. By one definition, anyone traveling more than 90 minutes one-way is a super commuter, which would include many Tokyo workers traveling in from the city's surrounding prefectures; another – perhaps more realistically – says it must be a distance of at least 150 kilometers. There is no firm data on how many long-distance commuters there are in the world, but it is estimated, for example, that around 300,000 Lebanese travel three hours by plane to work in the Persian Gulf. Around 3 percent of workers, or 80,000

UNIT 4 | Trains, Planes, and Automobiles

people, in Houston, Texas, commute for over 90 minutes, while 64,000 do so in New York, with Philadelphia – 160 kilometers away – being the largest home base.

The rise in remote working due to the coronavirus pandemic saw a large rise in the number of employees choosing to locate themselves far from their companies. Historically, super commuters tended to be senior <u>executives</u> in the tech industry, whose roles allowed them to carry out their work at home, traveling to the office only rarely. The pandemic, however, saw this privilege granted to a much wider range of workers, even from outside the tech sector. Around 5 million Americans moved after 2020 thanks to remote working, while more Australians moved out of major cities in 2021 than at any point in the last two decades.

One of those who benefited from the trend is Blaine Bassett, a marketing manager with a travel company based in San Francisco. Deciding to take himself far from the company's headquarters, where housing can be extremely expensive, he now rents a property in Lake Tahoe, a beautifully scenic location some 300 kilometers away on the California-Nevada border. Bassett had expected the move to be temporary, a way to spend a winter skiing in the mountains, but even with the end of the pandemic, his company has allowed him to continue with the same working arrangement. He comes to the office around two or three times a month by car.

Bassett says that this style of working does require planning. He can't go into the office at a moment's notice anymore and has to "check traffic times well in advance, leave at the crack of dawn and try to cram in as many in-person meetings into the day as possible." Another challenge is the absence of social opportunities with his colleagues and the lack of informal "water cooler talk" that can be a valuable source of new ideas and strategies. "Meetings are now much more intentional," Bassett acknowledges. "Building team culture is a bit harder than it used to be and it's tiring being in the car so much."

Unfortunately for would-be super commuters, the concerns Bassett refers to are also shared by a growing number of companies, which have begun to call workers back into the office. Prominent tech leaders like Elon Musk and finance executives like JP Morgan's Jamie Dimon are vocal critics of remote

27

working and have ordered their employees back into the office full-time. There is now a tension between remote workers enjoying their new lifestyles in pleasant, <u>rural</u> locations and the corporations that pay them. Does this mean super commuting is likely to decline over the coming years? Experts say it is possible but that it will certainly not die out altogether. For people like Blaine Bassett, the advantages are simply too great. "When I need a break or I have a one-on-one, I take calls while walking in the forest or down at the lake," he says. For a lifestyle like that, a long commute definitely seems worth it.

NOTES

spare a thought 思いを馳せる   **spacious** 広々とした   **not inconsiderable** 少なくない
compensate for 補う   **would-be** ～になろうと思っている，～志望の   **Persian Gulf** ペルシャ湾
privilege 特権   **at a moment's notice** 急に   **at the crack of dawn** 夜明けとともに（時間の速さを協調する表現）   **water cooler talk** おしゃべり，うわさ話（職場の休憩所などで交わされる会話）
intentional 意図的に   **vocal critic** 声高に批判する人

Reading Comprehension

Decide if each sentence is true or false.

1. [T / F]   David Bearce had always planned to become a super commuter.

2. [T / F]   Financially, Bearce does not lose out by commuting from Minneapolis.

3. [T / F]   The coronavirus pandemic opened super commuting to more types of workers.

4. [T / F]   Blaine Bassett has been super commuting for longer than he expected.

5. [T / F]   Some business leaders are critical of the rise in remote working.

UNIT 4 | Trains, Planes, and Automobiles

Finding Details

Write down the answer to each question.

1. What is the second definition of "super commuter" given in the article?

_____

2. How many Americans moved after 2020 due to the rise in remote working?

_____

3. Why might the lack of "water cooler talk" be a disadvantage for companies?

_____

Extend Your Vocabulary

Choose the correct word from the list to complete each sentence.

suburbs	accommodation	phenomenon	executive	rural

1. The family bought a nice house in the _____.

2. It is a _____ area but more convenient than you might imagine.

3. She is a successful _____ in a communications company.

4. Due to the festival, there was no _____ available in the town.

5. This _____ has not been studied in detail yet.

29

Summary

 1-39

Listen to the audio and fill in the spaces.

Traveling into Tokyo on a crowded morning train isn't something most people enjoy, but around the world there are workers for whom this would seem like a pretty easy (1) _____. Known as super commuters, these hardworking men and women travel much further to work, often taking cars and planes before even stepping foot on a city center train. Some do it out of choice, (2) _____ to live in the countryside where houses are larger and living costs lower; others find it is the best way to earn a living. The rise in remote working due to the coronavirus pandemic opened up the possibility of super commuting to a much larger (3) _____ of workers than before; but working from home has disadvantages as well as advantages to both (4) _____ and companies. Will super commuting survive if remote working (5) _____? Well, if you can take a work call while strolling beside a scenic lake, there are many people who would hope so.

UNIT 4 | Trains, Planes, and Automobiles

Expressing Your Opinion

→ Discussion

What do you think about the following statement? Think of two reasons for your opinion and share them with your classmates. Try to add details or examples and continue your conversation for as long as you can.

I would like to try super commuting in my future job.

5. Strongly Agree   4. Agree   3. Neither agree nor disagree
2. Disagree   1. Strongly disagree

Reason 1: _____

_____

_____

Reason 2: _____

_____

_____

→ Paragraph Writing

Finish this short paragraph about the opinion above. Give details or examples for your reasons.

I think / don't think that I would like to try super commuting. First, _____

_____

_____

_____

_____

_____

_____

_____

31

UNIT 5

Long Weekends

Should we work four days a week?

Introduction

Everybody enjoys the long weekend that comes along with a Monday national holiday, but how would it feel to have three days off every week? A growing number of workers are discovering the answer to that question as more and more firms experiment with introducing a four-day week. Can it be successful?

Activate Your Thinking

Think about the following questions and share your ideas with your classmates.

1. Which day of the week do you enjoy the most? Why?

   _____

   _____

2. Do you think people work too hard in Japan?

   _____

   _____

UNIT 5 | Long Weekends

Reading

Read the passage and check that you understand the underlined words.

Ask people which part of the week they are most looking forward to and the answer for most will surely be the weekend. So, how would they feel if, instead of having to get through five days of work before that happy moment arrived, they only had to wait four? Would this make them more satisfied with their lives? Would it mean they accomplished less in their jobs, or could they actually accomplish more? Once upon a time, these questions might have seemed pointless – who works only four days in a full-time job? But not anymore. Nowadays, a growing number of companies are experimenting with making the four-day week a reality. The outcome of these experiments could affect the entire future of work.

Much of the effort behind the trend is driven by a nonprofit organization associated with the University of Oxford called 4 Day Week Global. In 2022, it launched a worldwide effort to encourage firms to participate in a six-month trial in which each employee was given three days off a week. Under the recommended model, the workweek was reduced from 40 hours to 32 hours with salaries remaining the same as before. The nonprofit calls this the 100-80-100 system: workers receive 100 percent of their pay for 80 percent of the time and maintain 100 percent productivity.

The trial attracted several hundred companies around the world from a variety of sectors, including tech, finance, marketing, food retail, and even manufacturing. Almost all elected to implement the 100-80-100 model, accepting guidance and advice from 4 Day Week Global in order to introduce the change smoothly. As the trial proceeded, researchers from the nonprofit collaborated with academics to analyze the effects, focusing on key metrics such as employee satisfaction and mental health, number of sick days taken, staff retention and hiring rates, productivity and work rates, and overall business performance. The results were announced in early 2023.

Overwhelmingly, these results turned out to be positive. In the U.K., for example, more than 90 percent of the 61 firms who joined the experiment decided to continue it once the six months were over; 18 of them announced they would make the arrangement permanent. They reported higher levels of productivity, with business <u>revenues</u> remaining the same despite the reduced hours, and a 65 percent reduction in sick days. From the employee side, workers said they felt less stress and burnout and a better level of work-life balance.

CD 1-45

One company which participated in the trial was Kickstarter, a crowdfunding website based in New York. Its chief strategy officer, John Leland, was positive about the impact the four-day week was having on his business. As well as improving the firm's ability to retain its staff, it was coming up in hiring interviews as a competitive advantage, allowing the company to attract high-quality employees. For Joe O'Connor, CEO of 4 Day Week Global, this is a key factor in the trend spreading: "It's inevitable we'll see bigger companies doing this," he says. "This is my message to CEOs of big companies, where there's a huge amount of competition. The biggest risk isn't trying this out and it not working. Your biggest risk is your competitor doing it first."

CD 1-46

One place you might think would be reluctant to hear O'Connor's message is hardworking Japan, but even there a growing number of companies are offering their workers a four-day schedule. Hitachi, Fast Retailing, Mizuho, and Panasonic have all implemented the change, though, at the moment, the 100-80-100 model is not the system they have chosen. At Hitachi, workers are asked to make up the difference in work hours by staying longer at the office, while Mizuho said it would likely reduce workers' salaries. Even if these models are not ideal from the viewpoint of 4 Day Week Global, at least they offer workers a flexibility they did not enjoy in the past. This might be key in a country where birth rates are dropping in the face of a lack of support for new mothers and fathers.

CD 1-47

With all its advantages, therefore, could the four-day week become a norm? That might depend on the type of company. One participant in the U.K. trial that didn't react to it positively was an engineering firm called Allcap. Realizing that giving employees a three-day weekend wouldn't work, Allcap decided to offer one extra day off every two weeks. But even then, they ran into problems. As a manufacturer, their workflow was determined by orders

UNIT 5 | Long Weekends

coming in from customers, which usually had to be filled by a certain
deadline. It was hard, therefore, to structure an effective four-day schedule. 65
"As opposed to 10 normal workdays, we found that employees would have
nine extreme ones.... We also struggled to find cover for an employee on
their rest day." Reluctantly, the firm abandoned the trial two months early.

1-48

The four-day week might not work everywhere. Nevertheless, such is its
popularity with employees – 92 percent support its introduction at their 70
workplace, according to a recent Qualtrics survey – that it seems inevitable
the idea will continue to spread. Soon you might not have to wait for a
Monday national holiday to enjoy a three-day weekend. It could happen
every week.

NOTES

associated with に関連する   **entire** 全体の   **elect** 選択する   **metric** 指標   **retention rate**
定着率   **overwhelmingly** 圧倒的に   **burnout** 燃え尽き症候群   **competitive advantage** 競争
優位性   **reluctant** 嫌がる，抵抗がある   **determined by** 〜によって決定される   **as opposed to**
〜とは対照的に，〜ではなく

Reading Comprehension

▶ **Decide if each sentence is true or false.**

1. [T / F]   Under the 100-80-100 model, companies have to accept their
   employees achieving less at work.

2. [T / F]   The results of the 4 Day Week Global trial were measured with
   data.

3. [T / F]   Kickstarter says that a four-day week is helping their recruitment.

4. [T / F]   Japanese firms are following the model recommended by 4 Day
   Week Global.

5. [T / F]   Allcap didn't finish the six-month trial.

35

Finding Details

Write down the answer to each question.

1. How much did business revenues decrease during the six-month trial?

_____

2. Why does Joe O'Connor say there is a risk to big companies if they don't try the four-day week?

_____

3. What type of company didn't react positively to the four-day week trial in the U.K.?

_____

Extend Your Vocabulary

Choose the correct word from the list to complete each sentence.

accomplish	productivity	implement	collaborate	revenue

1. I plan to _____ with a research team based in London.

2. If every employee can increase their _____, we will be able to lower our prices.

3. I never imagined we would be able to _____ so much together.

4. Thanks to your hard work, _____ has increased by 20 percent this year.

5. We plan to _____ a new marketing strategy from April.

UNIT 5 | Long Weekends

Summary

 1-49

Listen to the audio and fill in the spaces.

Almost everybody looks forward to the weekend when work finishes and relaxation begins. But a growing number of companies are (1) _____ with the idea of bringing the weekend forward a day each week, giving their workers three days off instead of two. The trend is being driven by a nonprofit organization called 4 Day Week Global, which launched a (2) _____ trial of the 100-80-100 model of working; that is, 100 percent salary for 80 percent work hours with 100 percent productivity. The trial was greeted positively by almost all of the firms that (3) _____. Business revenues did not decrease while employees reported feeling happier and less stressed. Although the four-day week might not work for every company, particularly those in the (4) _____ sector, its popularity with both managers and workers means it seems certain to (5) _____. Soon we might not have to wait for a Monday national holiday to enjoy a three-day weekend.

Expressing Your Opinion

→ Discussion

What do you think about the following statement? Think of two reasons for your opinion and share them with your classmates. Try to add details or examples and continue your conversation for as long as you can.

Large firms in Japan should introduce a four-day week.

5. Strongly Agree   4. Agree   3. Neither agree nor disagree

2. Disagree   1. Strongly disagree

Reason 1: _____

_____

_____

Reason 2: _____

_____

_____

→ Paragraph Writing

Finish this short paragraph about the opinion above. Give details or examples for your reasons.

I think / don't think that large firms in Japan should introduce a four-day week.

First, _____

_____

_____

_____

_____

_____

_____

UNIT 6

Tourism
Is it a blessing or a curse?

Introduction

Tourism is a huge global industry, bringing significant economic value to the destinations that attract the most visitors. But it has a dark side too, with overcrowding, noise, and litter just some of the environmental problems it can bring. How can we maximize the benefits of tourism and minimize the downsides?

Activate Your Thinking

Think about the following questions and share your ideas with your classmates.

1. Do you like traveling? What is the most interesting trip you have taken?

_____

_____

2. If you could visit any place in the world, where would you go and why?

_____

_____

Reading

🎵 1-51~56

Read the passage and check that you understand the underlined words.

🎵 1-51

Lines so long you can't even see the place you're trying to enter; buses so packed you can hardly breathe; crowds so tightly jammed into the streets it takes half an hour to walk a hundred meters: if you've tried visiting Kyoto during cherry blossom season, you will know exactly how these experiences feel. And Japan's ancient capital is hardly unique when it comes to popularity with domestic and overseas tourists. Try visiting destinations like Hong Kong, Paris, Rome, or London during peak times. It can take half a day just to get inside a museum.

🎵 1-52

Mass tourism is what we call in English a "double-edged sword." That is, a situation with both positive and negative aspects. A sharp edge on one side of your sword makes it an effective weapon; a sharp edge on both sides and you might cut your own arm off. Let's start with the positives. According to the World Travel and Tourism Council, tourism contributed 10.4 percent of global GDP in 2019 and supported 334 million jobs, one-tenth of global employment. (During the coronavirus pandemic in 2020, this dropped to 5.5 percent, leading to the loss of at least 62 million jobs.) For some developing countries in particular, tourism is not just an important part of the economy, it is practically the only one, the sector upon which everything else depends. In the Caribbean islands of Antigua and Barbuda, for instance, fully 91 percent of jobs are related to the tourism industry while in Macau and the Maldives the figure is well over 60 percent. With an estimated total value of 9.2 trillion US dollars, it is not surprising governments around the world are trying to gain as large a portion of the pie as possible. Japan, for example, aims to attract 60 million inbound tourists a year by 2030, a 50 percent increase from its current goal.

🎵 1-53

Tourism has other upsides too alongside its economic value. The revenue created can be used to conserve important historical and cultural landmarks, maintaining their beauty for future generations to enjoy. The Taj Mahal in India is a good example of this. Foreign tourists pay 1,100 rupees ($13) for entrance to the monument, the money contributing to a public fund which keeps the beautiful marble mausoleum in pristine condition. Without the money, this magnificent world heritage site might have been left to fade away. Another advantage is its role in fostering international exchange and understanding. In a world that often seems divided among political or cultural lines, interaction between different peoples is one thing that can help to unite us. As the American writer Mark Twain once said, "Travel is fatal to prejudice, bigotry, and narrow-mindedness."

When tourism does not lead to positive outcomes, it is often due to the numbers of visitors involved. While locals might welcome tourists for the income they bring, they can also tire of the constant congestion, noise, and litter that arrive alongside. Then there are the cultural misunderstandings. Tourists rarely intend to cause trouble when they visit, but sometimes ignorance of local customs can cause irritation and stress. One destination that knows these problems well is Venice, the beautiful Italian city of canals, palaces, and winding medieval streets. Tourists are the lifeblood of thousands of hotels, restaurants, and shops, but the city's narrow streets and ancient buildings are ill-suited to the millions of people who visit each year. Already under threat from rising sea levels due to climate change, Venice sometimes appears to be drowning in people as well as water. A particular problem is the huge cruise ships that dock at its harbors, spewing out thousands of passengers at a time. Since they do not stay at hotels, their financial contribution to the city is limited; in 2016, locals took to the canals in fishing boats to block the passage of six cruise ships, shouting "No grandi navi" (No big ships).

Along with noise and litter, tourism can bring other kinds of environmental pollution too. It can damage delicate ecosystems through the development of resorts and transport infrastructure. It can place pressure on local resources of water and energy, particularly in small island nations where supplies are limited. It also increases carbon dioxide emissions, not least from the airplanes that constantly fly passengers back and forth.

The pros and cons of tourism mean that a balance has to be struck between economic benefit and environmental cost. Some popular destinations, including the Taj Mahal and Peru's Machu Picchu, have begun restricting visitor numbers to reduce the strain on local infrastructure and avoid damaging the site itself. Other countries have begun to encourage so-called "sustainable tourism," which focuses on conserving the environment and supporting local communities. In the Bwindi National Park in Uganda, home to endangered mountain gorillas, visitors help with conservation efforts through the money they pay. In Bhutan, meanwhile, tourists pay a daily fee that not only includes necessary expenses like accommodation, hiking equipment, and licensed tour guides, but also contributes directly to the country's free healthcare and education systems. Sustainable tourism is also known as "responsible tourism." In the end, taking responsibility for the impact of one's own visit may be the key to ensuring that tourism's double-edged sword only cuts on the side it's supposed to.

NOTES

jammed into 詰め込まれている　**sector** 部門　**portion** 部分　**marble mausoleum** 大理石の陵墓　**pristine condition** 完璧な状態，初期の状態　**fade away** 消え去る　**bigotry** 偏屈　**narrow-mindedness** 偏狭さ　**ignorance** 無知　**winding** 曲がりくねった　**lifeblood** 活力源　**dock** 停泊する　**spew out** 吐き出す　**pros and cons** プラス面とマイナス面　**strike a balance** 上手くバランスをとる　**strain** 負担

Reading Comprehension

Decide if each sentence is true or false.

1. [T / F]　One in ten jobs worldwide is related to the tourism industry.

2. [T / F]　The writer Mark Twain was not a fan of traveling to other countries.

3. [T / F]　Venice is a good example of the pros and cons of tourism.

4. [T / F]　Cruise ship tourists probably contribute less to Venice's economy than ordinary visitors.

5. [T / F]　Sustainable tourism is only useful for protecting endangered animals.

UNIT 6 | Tourism

Finding Details

Write down the answer to each question.

1. How many jobs were lost in the tourism sector in 2020?

_____

2. What is Japan's current goal for the number of overseas tourists visiting the country?

_____

3. What do the Taj Mahal and Machu Picchu have in common with regard to tourism policies?

_____

Extend Your Vocabulary

Choose the correct word from the list to complete each sentence.

conserve	foster	interaction	congestion	ecosystem

1. The city discussed plans to reduce traffic _____ in the streets.

2. The event should help to _____ a spirit of cooperation in the community.

3. The delicate _____ of the rainforest must be protected at all costs.

4. The scientists observed the _____ between the male and female gorillas.

5. The organization was working to _____ areas of natural beauty.

43

Summary

 1-57

Listen to the audio and fill in the spaces.

Tourism is a double-edged sword. The advantages are mostly (1) _____. Over one-tenth of global GDP is generated by the travel industry, with millions of jobs dependent on the money spent by tourists at their (2) _____. For some countries, in fact, it is practically their only source of revenue. There are other advantages too. The income can be used to protect important monuments or areas of natural beauty, and the interaction it encourages between people of different cultures can help to foster international cooperation and friendship. The (3) _____ of tourism tend to come when the number of visitors is simply too great for the destination to handle, with Venice being a classic example of a small city that is frequently overwhelmed by the crowds (4) _____ into its narrow streets. Recently, the idea of "responsible tourism" has been gaining attention. A sense of (5) _____ is the one thing all tourists should have.

UNIT 6 Tourism

Expressing Your Opinion

→ Discussion

What do you think about the following statement? Think of two reasons for your opinion and share them with your classmates. Try to add details or examples and continue your conversation for as long as you can.

Japan should encourage more overseas tourists to visit.

5. Strongly Agree   4. Agree   3. Neither agree nor disagree
2. Disagree   1. Strongly disagree

Reason 1: _____

_____

_____

Reason 2: _____

_____

_____

→ Paragraph Writing

Finish this short paragraph about the opinion above. Give details or examples for your reasons.

I think / don't think that Japan should encourage more overseas tourists to visit.

First, _____

_____

_____

_____

_____

_____

45

UNIT 7

Agony of Uncertainty

Is it better to know what will happen?

Introduction

Which is worse: to know that something bad *is* going to happen to you or that something bad *might* happen to you? Scientists have conducted experiments to investigate this question, and the answer can be traced all the way back to our lives in primitive times. Which is it?

Activate Your Thinking

Think about the following questions and share your ideas with your classmates.

1. Are you the kind of person who worries about things? What kind of things do you worry about?

   _____

   _____

2. Do you like to know what will happen or are you happy not being certain?

   _____

   _____

UNIT 7 | Agony of Uncertainty

Reading

🎧 1-59～65

Read the passage and check that you understand the underlined words.

🎧 1-59

Imagine you were given three options: (1) You are not going to receive an electric shock; (2) You are definitely going to receive an electric shock; (3) You might receive an electric shock. It's probably safe to say you'd go with option (1). But what if you only had choices (2) and (3)? Which one would give you the most mental anxiety? Is it more stressful to know that something bad *is* going to happen or that something bad *might* happen? 5

🎧 1-60

Believe it or not, researchers know the answer to this question, and the reason they do so is that they have actually tried it out – with electric shocks. Sometimes the path to knowledge can be painful. A team from University College London recruited 45 volunteers to play a computer game in which 10 they had to turn over digital rocks, some of which had snakes hiding under them. Every time the players turned over a rock with a snake, they received a mild but painful electric shock on the hand. The game provided a way for the players to gradually get better at predicting where the snakes were hiding, but they could never do so with complete certainty. As the 15 participants turned over rocks one by one, the researchers monitored their stress levels with a variety of sensitive equipment.

🎧 1-61

The researchers found that when players were confident the rock they had to turn over concealed a snake, their stress levels were significantly lower than when they were not sure. In other words, the knowledge they *might* get an 20 electric shock was more stressful than the knowledge they definitely *would* get one. "Our experiment allows us to draw conclusions about the effect of uncertainty on stress," said Archy de Berker, the head of the study. "It turns out it's much worse not knowing."

🎧 1-62

The finding is interesting because it extends beyond the context of the study 25 itself. There are many occasions when we find ourselves fearing a negative outcome from a situation that we have little control over: Did I fail that test I just took? Will this train delay mean I am late for class? Will my favorite sports team win the game? In all these cases, it is the uncertainty that causes

47

the most stress. Most likely, we have <u>evolved</u> to respond this way from primitive times as a mechanism to keep ourselves safe: that rock near our cave might actually have a snake beneath it so let's make sure we're ready to react when we turn it over. But that doesn't mean we can't conquer our anxiety if we try. When nervous about an outcome, psychologists recommend thinking of the worst-case scenario and imagining it will definitely happen. Often you find it is not as bad as you feared.

CD 1-63

Knowing *why* we think negatively can help us to <u>overcome</u> feelings of unhappiness or anxiety. Psychologists are aware of a phenomenon known as "negative bias," which is caused by our brains having a naturally greater sensitivity to bad news rather than good. In a study conducted by John Cacioppo of the University of Chicago, participants were shown pictures known to arouse positive feelings (like a pizza or a beautiful sports car), negative feelings (a dead cat or a badly injured face), and neutral feelings (a plate, a hair dryer). He measured electrical impulses in the brain's cerebral cortex that reflect the magnitude of information processing taking place. What he found was there was a greater increase in electrical activity when <u>subjects</u> viewed the <u>unpleasant</u> images compared to the positive or neutral ones, indicating that the brain reacts more strongly to negative stimuli.

CD 1-64

This too has implications outside the study itself. It explains why we tend to remember traumatic events more than pleasant ones, recall insults more than praise, and have negative thoughts more frequently than positive ones. For example, you might have been having a good day at school when one of your classmates makes an accidentally hurtful comment. When you come home and someone asks you how your day was, you reply that it was awful because of that one comment, even though everything else went fine. Another example would be how we often recall humiliating events years after they happened to us. We can actually find ourselves physically cringing with embarrassment, despite it having no impact on our current lives. This could also explain the phenomenon of post-traumatic stress disorder, or PTSD – a condition caused by an event that was so stressful at the time it still creates real and debilitating mental pain many years later.

CD 1-65

Overcoming negative bias is not easy, but there are certain methods we can use to avoid falling into a negative mindset. Psychologists recommend

UNIT 7 | Agony of Uncertainty

keeping a notebook of positive events that occurred in the day or things you
felt grateful for. They also tell us to recognize when our thoughts are turning
dark and make a deliberate effort to stop them. Turn on a TV show that will
make you laugh or play a game that will occupy your attention – anything to
keep you from turning over the same negative thoughts in your head. Above
all, remember it's not strange to overreact to an unpleasant occurrence. It's
the way our brains were designed.

65

70

NOTES

worst-case scenario 最悪のケース　**bias** バイアス，偏見　**arouse** 喚起する　**electrical**
impulses 電気インパルス　**cerebral cortex** 大脳皮質　**stimuli** 刺激［stimulus の複数形］
implication 意味，意義　**traumatic** トラウマになるような　**recall** 思い出す　**cringe** 身がすくむ
post-traumatic stress disorder (PTSD) 心的外傷後ストレス障害　**debilitating** 衰弱させる
turn over thoughts in your head 頭の中で繰り返し考える　**overreact** 過剰に反応する

Reading Comprehension

Decide if each sentence is true or false.

1. [T / F]　The answer to the first question in paragraph one is option (2).

2. [T / F]　By playing the game, participants could always guess where the
snakes were.

3. [T / F]　If we want to overcome our anxiety, we should avoid imagining
the worst-case scenario.

4. [T / F]　Subjects in John Cacioppo's experiment reacted most strongly
to the negative images.

5. [T / F]　Negative bias might be a cause of PTSD.

49

Finding Details

Write down the answer to each question.

1. In the game, in what situation did the players receive an electric shock?

_____

2. How did John Cacioppo measure how the brain reacted to different kinds of images?

_____

3. What is the purpose of turning on a funny TV show in the context of negative bias?

_____

Extend Your Vocabulary

Choose the correct word from the list to complete each sentence.

anxiety	monitor	contexts	evolve	subjects

1. The _____ in the experiment were paid a small amount of money.

2. She managed to overcome her _____ about the test.

3. How did our brains _____ to make us so intelligent?

4. We can _____ the results in real-time through this program.

5. The study had implications in a variety of _____.

UNIT 7 Agony of Uncertainty

Summary

 1-66

Listen to the audio and fill in the spaces.

Which would cause you the most mental anxiety: to know you *are* going to receive an electric shock or to know you *might* receive one? Scientists have actually studied this question (1) _____ and the answer they found was that not knowing whether something bad will happen causes more stress. Our brains probably evolved to (2) _____ this way from primitive times as a mechanism to keep ourselves safe, and it still has an impact on how we think and behave. The same is true of another mental phenomenon known as "negative bias," which has also been (3) _____ in experiments. A psychologist named John Cacioppo (4) _____ that our brains react more strongly to unpleasant images than to pleasant or neutral ones. The good news is we can overcome these (5) _____ tendencies by doing things like writing down our positive experiences or distracting ourselves when we start having dark thoughts.

51

Expressing Your Opinion

→ Discussion

What do you think about the following statement? Think of two reasons for your opinion and share them with your classmates. Try to add details or examples and continue your conversation for as long as you can.

Society should put more emphasis on the importance of mental health.

5. Strongly Agree   4. Agree   3. Neither agree nor disagree
2. Disagree   1. Strongly disagree

Reason 1: _____

_____

_____

Reason 2: _____

_____

_____

→ Paragraph Writing

Finish this short paragraph about the opinion above. Give details or examples for your reasons.

I think / don't think that society should put more emphasis on the importance of mental health. First, _____

_____

_____

_____

_____

_____

_____

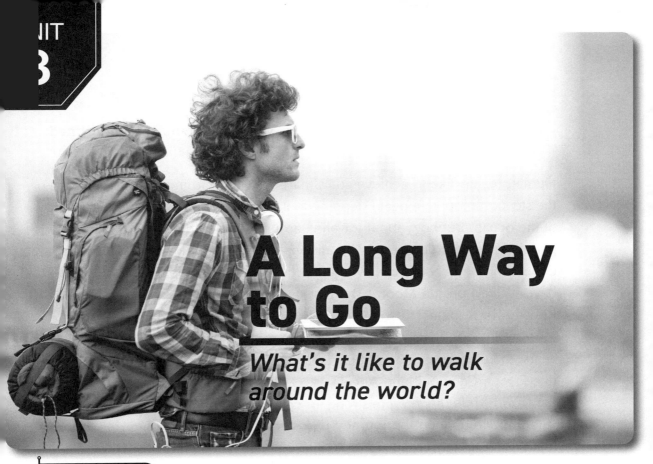

A Long Way to Go

What's it like to walk around the world?

Introduction

Lots of people like to travel around the world but very few have ever done so on foot. What made ordinary men and women like Tom Turcich and Angela Maxwell decide to leave their homes and set off on a journey that would take years to complete? And what did they learn from their experience?

Activate Your Thinking

Think about the following questions and share your ideas with your classmates.

1. Do you like walking or hiking? What is the longest walk you have ever done?

   _____

   _____

2. If you had time and money, would you like to travel around the world without using airplanes?

   _____

   _____

> **Reading**   🎧 1-68~73

Read the passage and check that you understand the underlined words.

🎧 1-68

Human beings like to achieve goals that seem close to impossible: climbing the steepest mountain peak, stepping foot on the Moon, diving to the bottom of the ocean. But how about traveling around the world on foot? How many people have ever done that? The answer appears to be between 10 and 15,
5 depending on exactly how we <u>define</u> the feat. (By comparison, 12 people have walked on the Moon.) The first person to claim the achievement was Konstantin Rengarten from Belarus, who is said to have completed the journey in four years and one month from 1894 to 1898. In more recent years, there have been men such as Kevin Carr and Tom Turcich and women
10 like Ffyona Campbell and Angela Maxwell. Some walked their way around the world while others were strong, or crazy, enough to run it. Kevin Carr, for example, completed the journey in just 19 months by running one to two marathons per day for a total of 26,232 kilometers.

🎧 1-69

While you can understand the motivation for wanting to travel and see the
15 world, there are easier ways to do it than on foot. So, what motivates people to spend years of their lives doing something that surely can't be anything other than <u>exhausting</u>, lonely, and even dangerous?

🎧 1-70

For Tom Turcich, the journey began in trauma when one of his closest friends was killed in a jet ski accident at the age of 16. Stunned by the death of the
20 brightest and kindest person he knew, he began questioning his own life and what it meant. What would he do with his time on this planet? Would he stay in the small town he grew up in and get a regular job, or go away and do something extraordinary? He was only 17 when he made up his mind to walk around the world, but he spent eight years saving money and making
25 plans before he finally set off. He left his hometown in New Jersey on the east coast of the U.S. with a tent, a sleeping bag, a camera, six pairs of socks, four pairs of underwear, a pair of shorts, a pair of pants, two shirts, a jacket, and some waterproof shoes, leaving behind a supportive dad and an anxious mom as he headed down the road toward South America. When he reached
30 Texas some months later, he picked up an abandoned dog whom he named

54

UNIT 8 | **A Long Way to Go**

Savannah. Savannah became his companion for the rest of the journey.

CD 1-71

It took Tom seven years to complete his trip, having traveled through 38 countries and walked for 45,000 kilometers. There were occasional dangers along the way – in Panama City his backpack was stolen at knifepoint and on the Turkish border he was questioned on suspicion of being a terrorist – but mostly he met kindness and a helping hand. He describes his first two years as a kind of meditation, his mind cleaning itself of all his worries and regrets. In the Atacama Desert of Chile, he lay under the starry sky and felt "a simple sense of existing. You're just a small creature in the universe. It was just peace." As he grew happier with himself, he became more social, learning enough French, Russian, Turkish, and Italian to allow him to communicate with local people. He made lifelong friends in Iceland and, on the final leg of his journey in North America, met a young woman who now lives with him in Seattle. Settling back down after so long on the road was not easy, but Tom is learning to adapt to a normal life once more. His father says he recognizes how much his son has grown: "He sees the world so differently. He's been to places where people with zero money work all week to add a cinder block to their house, and they would share all they had with him. To see that is a life-changer."

CD 1-72

Tom's story shares many of the same elements as that of another world walker, Angela Maxwell, who recently returned from her own six-and-a-half-year adventure. Angela's decision to leave her home in Oregon did not come from loss or trauma – she was a successful business owner in a relationship – but, like Tom, she was searching for something more in her life, "a deeper connection with nature and people." As a young woman, there were even more risks to her journey, and indeed a sexual assault by a nomad in Mongolia made her consider abandoning her quest. But on the whole the kindness she received from strangers made her appreciative of the basic goodness of human beings. She learned beekeeping in Georgia, camel handling in Mongolia, and traditional cooking in Italian villages. She chopped wood in New Zealand, handed out food to the homeless in Italy, and stayed in a mountain hut with an old lady in Vietnam.

CD 1-73

Walking around the world might be too great an adventure for most people. But one lesson that both Tom and Angela learned on their journey is something you don't need to travel far to understand. As Angela said: "Walking has taught me that everything and everyone has a story to share, and we just have to be willing to listen."

NOTES

feat 偉業　　**make up one's mind** 思い切る，決定する　　**knifepoint** ナイフを突きつけられて [robbed at gunpoint などで同じ表現を使う]　　**meditation** 瞑想，メディテーション　　**settle down** 定住する，住居を定める　　**cinder block** 軽量コンクリートブロック　　**element** 要素　　**sexual assault** 性的暴行　　**nomad** 遊牧民　　**quest** 探求　　**appreciative** 感謝の

Reading Comprehension

Decide if each sentence is true or false.

1. [T / F]　Kevin Carr ran rather than walked around the world.

2. [T / F]　Tom Turcich set off on his journey when he was just 17 years of age.

3. [T / F]　Tom became more social as his journey went on.

4. [T / F]　Meeting people much poorer than him changed Tom's view on life.

5. [T / F]　Angela Maxwell decided to leave home after a relationship ended.

Finding Details

Write down the answer to each question.

1. What tragic event made Tom Turcich decide to walk around the world?

   _____

2. Who was Tom's traveling partner for most of his journey?

   _____

3. What lesson did walking around the world teach Angela Maxwell?

   _____

UNIT 8 | A Long Way to Go

Extend Your Vocabulary

Choose the correct word from the list to complete each sentence.

| define | exhausting | suspicion | regret | recognize |

1. The man was arrested on _____ of murder.

2. Hiking up that mountain was completely _____ for me.

3. We have to _____ how important this project is for the company.

4. How do we _____ this word?

5. The one _____ I have is not traveling more when I was younger.

Summary

🎧 1-74

Listen to the audio and fill in the spaces.

There are many kinds of adventures people can have, but walking all the way around the world has to be one of the greatest. Few have (1) _____ this incredible feat, but two people who have managed it are Tom Turcich and Angela Maxwell. Both young people set off on their long journey in search of some new (2) _____ for their lives. Tom felt the first two years of his trip were a kind of meditation as he learned to accept himself and put away the small (3) _____ of his life. His experiences in meeting people with few possessions and little money changed him, giving him a (4) _____ perspective on life. Angela too returned as a different person, having shared (5) _____ with strangers all over the world. As she says, "Walking has taught me that everything and everyone has a story to share, and we just have to be willing to listen."

57

Expressing Your Opinion

→ Discussion

What do you think about the following statement? Think of two reasons for your opinion and share them with your classmates. Try to add details or examples and continue your conversation for as long as you can.

It is important to travel overseas when you are young.

5. Strongly Agree   4. Agree   3. Neither agree nor disagree
2. Disagree   1. Strongly disagree

Reason 1: _____

_____

_____

Reason 2: _____

_____

_____

→ Paragraph Writing

Finish this short paragraph about the opinion above. Give details or examples for your reasons.

I think / don't think that it is important to travel overseas when you are young.

First, _____

_____

_____

_____

_____

_____

_____

58

UNIT 9

Lost Cities

Are they myth or reality?

Introduction

In the shadows of time, hidden beneath shifting sands, thick jungles, or rolling seas, lay the remains of ancient civilizations that once thrived but then faded into darkness. What are these lost cities and why do they hold such fascination for us? Did they even exist in the first place?

Activate Your Thinking

Think about the following questions and share your ideas with your classmates.

1. Do you know of any famous lost cities in the world? What are they?

_____

_____

2. What are some legends or myths you have heard from Japan or overseas?

_____

_____

59

Reading

Read the passage and check that you understand the underlined words.

Imagine you are an explorer from 200 years ago hungry for fame and fortune. You have heard the stories: El Dorado, the city of gold hidden within the Andes mountains; Atlantis, the island civilization drowned in a catastrophic flood; Troy, the ancient enemy of Greece destroyed in an epic 10-year war. At one time, these cities ruled empires, collecting riches from lands far and wide. Surely, they are still out there somewhere. Can you be the one who finds them?

We don't know how many explorers set out to search for the cities of El Dorado, Atlantis, and Troy, as well as others like them. What we do know is that of the three cities, only one has been found. The others might not have even existed in the first place. Let's start with the most famous: Atlantis, the inspiration for many a Hollywood movie, including Disney's *Little Mermaid*. Was this ever a real place? Where did the legend come from?

Strangely, for a land that has had such an impact on world culture, the evidence for Atlantis is extremely thin. It was actually a story told by the Greek philosopher Plato, who spoke of a powerful island kingdom whose ships sailed to every corner of the world. Far more technologically advanced than their neighbors, they made war on the Mediterranean nations and enslaved their peoples. In doing so, however, they angered the gods, who sent an earthquake and flood to destroy them. Atlantis disappeared beneath the waves.

Plato meant the story of Atlantis as a warning to his home city of Athens, which was aiming to create its own empire. The tale, however, was never real and few people took it to be so at the time. It was only picked up later by Roman historians, who wondered if part of the story might be true. Almost certainly it was not, and despite multiple expeditions over the centuries, no trace of Atlantis has ever been found.

The legend of El Dorado has more substance to it. It was first reported in the

UNIT 9 | Lost Cities

16th century when Spanish explorers conquered the Inca Empire of South America. They heard rumors of a tribal chief who presided over an <u>annual</u> ceremony at Lake Guatavita in which gold was thrown into the water to satisfy the gods. The Spanish had found enough gold among the Inca to consider the story credible and it was not long before they reached Lake Guatavita and began to drain it in search of treasure. The first expedition in 1545 managed to reduce the water level by three meters, uncovering approximately $100,000 worth of gold pieces at modern values. Further expeditions over the next 200 years lowered the water level further, but accidents and mistakes prevented the work being carried out successfully. In 1965, the Colombian government made further exploration of the lake illegal.

CD 1-81

The tribal chief, whom the Spanish nicknamed El Dorado or "the golden one," might have been a real person, but over time the legend grew into the idea of an entire city made from gold hidden somewhere in the Andes mountains. Journeys to find the city, however, led nowhere. Like Atlantis, it likely never existed. So that leaves the third famous lost city, Troy, the ancient capital of a Turkish empire that fell into war with the Greeks. The legend of Troy comes from the Greek poet, Homer, who wrote of a Trojan prince falling in love with a beautiful Greek queen named Helen and taking her back to his home. In retaliation, Helen's husband, King Agamemnon, gathered together a great army and sailed to Troy, laying siege to the large, walled city for 10 years. Unable to break through, the Greeks finally took the city by trickery by presenting it with a giant wooden horse inside which Greek soldiers were secretly hidden. The soldiers sneaked out at night and opened the city gates, allowing the Greek army to pour through. Troy was conquered and destroyed.

CD 1-82

Homer's tale is an incredibly powerful piece of writing, but the Trojan War is not mentioned in any other historical documents. One man who believed it, however, was a German businessman called Heinrich Schliemann, who traveled to Hisarlik on the west coast of Turkey in the late 19th century to search for the lost city. Schliemann discovered many artefacts, including jewelry, which he claimed must have belonged to Helen herself. Further investigation showed the artefacts dated from the 13th century BC, which was more recent than the setting of Homer's tale. Nevertheless, historians do

believe Schliemann had found the ancient city of Troy, even though it was
not of a particularly impressive size. Arrow heads discovered at the site
suggest it was the scene of warfare, and the consensus today is that Greek
armies did raid there during the long struggle for dominance in the region.
Homer may have taken his inspiration from a real event, exaggerating it into
a long, epic tale.

CD 1-83

El Dorado, Atlantis, and Troy are just three of the world's lost cities. There are
many others, some of which have been found and others not. Our fascination
with them is really a fascination with ourselves and our own future. If these
great cities thrived and then disappeared, could the same happen to our
own? It is a question never more important than today.

NOTES

catastrophic 壊滅的な **epic** 壮絶な **enslave** 奴隷にする **substance** 真実味，本質 **Inca Empire** インカ帝国［南アメリカのアンデス地域における広大で洗練された先コロンブス期の文明］
tribal chief 部族長 **preside over** 主宰する **credible** 信憑性のある **drain**（水を）抜く
retaliation 報復 **lay siege to** ～を包囲する **sneak out** こっそり抜け出す **artefact** 遺物
raid 襲撃する **thrive** 繁栄する

Reading Comprehension

Decide if each sentence is true or false.

1. [T / F]   None of the cities of El Dorado, Atlantis, and Troy really existed.

2. [T / F]   Plato's story of Atlantis was really about his own city of Athens.

3. [T / F]   El Dorado was originally meant as a person rather than a place.

4. [T / F]   Items discovered by Heinrich Schliemann in Hisarlik dated back
to the same time period as Homer's tale of Troy.

5. [T / F]   Troy did exist, but it was not as large as Homer's story suggested.

UNIT 9 | Lost Cities

Finding Details

Write down the answer to each question.

1. What did Atlantis and Athens have in common, according to Plato?

_____

2. Why did the Greeks start a war with Troy in Homer's story?

_____

3. What question about ourselves do the world's lost cities bring to mind?

_____

Extend Your Vocabulary

Choose the correct word from the list to complete each sentence.

| civilization | expedition | trace | annual | exaggerate |

1. The _____ fireworks display is one of the highlights of my hometown.

2. This ancient _____ was more advanced than we first thought.

3. The police were not able to find a single _____ of the criminal.

4. This _____ is aimed at discovering new plants in the rainforest.

5. The story is fantastic already, so there is no need to _____ it.

63

Summary

Listen to the audio and fill in the spaces.

For centuries, explorers have dreamed of finding lost cities. Whether it is Atlantis, the powerful island that (1) _____ beneath the sea, El Dorado, the Andes city of gold, or Troy, the ancient enemy of Greece, there are places in the world so shrouded in mystery we don't know whether they truly (2) _____ in the first place. In the case of Atlantis, there appears little chance it was ever real. It was simply a story told by Plato as a (3) _____ to his own city of Athens. El Dorado has more (4) _____ in fact, but, if it did exist, it might have been a person rather than a place. Troy, however, was likely a real kingdom, though not as powerful as in the story told by Homer. Its remains were discovered by a German businessman in the 19th century. The world's lost cities remind us that nothing is (5) _____. Civilizations that once thrived can disappear beneath sand and water. Could the same thing happen to our own?

UNIT 9 | Lost Cities

Expressing Your Opinion

→ Discussion

What do you think about the following statement? Think of two reasons for your opinion and share them with your classmates. Try to add details or examples and continue your conversation for as long as you can.

> One day our own great cities will disappear.

5. Strongly Agree　　**4. Agree**　　**3. Neither agree nor disagree**

2. Disagree　　**1. Strongly disagree**

Reason 1: _____

_____

_____

Reason 2: _____

_____

_____

→ Paragraph Writing

Finish this short paragraph about the opinion above. Give details or examples for your reasons.

I think / don't think that one day our own great cities will disappear. First, _____

_____

_____

_____

_____

_____

_____

_____

65

UNIT 10

An Ordinary Hero

How did one man stop World War III?

Introduction

It sounds like a Hollywood movie, but sometimes it only takes one person to save the world. If Stanislav Petrov had reacted differently on the night of September 26, 1983, the world could have been plunged into a nuclear war. What did Petrov do and why?

Activate Your Thinking

Think about the following questions and share your ideas with your classmates.

1. Who is your biggest hero and why?

   _____

   _____

2. What do you know about the Cold War between the United States and the Soviet Union?

   _____

   _____

UNIT 10 | An Ordinary Hero

Reading

Read the passage and check that you understand the underlined words.

The American essayist Ralph Waldo Emerson once wrote, "A hero is no braver than an ordinary man, but he is brave five minutes longer." Emerson was referring to the quality of perseverance in the face of danger, of continuing to act courageously when everything tells you to give up. In the case of Stanislav Petrov, however, there is a literal truth to this famous quotation. Petrov's five minutes of bravery probably saved the world from nuclear Armageddon.

To understand Petrov's story, we have to step back in time to 1983, the height of the Cold War between the United States and the Soviet Union. For almost 40 years after the end of the Second World War, the two superpowers had been locked in a struggle for supremacy on the global stage. On one side was America and its allies, promoting Western-style capitalism and (for the most part) democratic ideals; on the other was the Soviet Union, a communist, totalitarian state seeking to spread its influence beyond the Eastern European countries already under its control. Already, the two countries had come close to war. In Korea (1950 – 1953) and Vietnam (1954 – 1975), they had given military support to opposing sides in long, terrible conflicts; and in 1962, they had come to the brink of disaster when the U.S. discovered Soviet missiles in Cuba, less than 150 kilometers from the American coast. Only last-minute, secret negotiations between U.S. President John F. Kennedy and Soviet leader Nikita Khrushchev had prevented war from breaking out.

In 1983, the superpowers were involved in another indirect conflict in Afghanistan, which had been invaded by the Soviets in 1979. Tension was high between the two sides, and with each country possessing enough nuclear weapons to destroy the other 10 times over, the potential for catastrophe was real. And here begins the story of Stanislav Petrov, a young military officer in the Soviet Union. Petrov worked within an underground command center near Moscow, which was responsible for the country's early warning systems for incoming missile attacks. The system was designed

67

to detect launches of American nuclear missiles and give the Soviet military time to launch a counterstrike before the missiles hit. Petrov's role was to monitor the alert system. With the Soviet Union's very existence at stake, it was a job given only to the most trusted officers.

CD 1-89

35 At approximately 12:15 AM on the night of September 26, 1983, the system's alarms suddenly rang out, indicating the detection of an incoming missile launch from the United States. Petrov's shock was so great that for a few moments he couldn't even move. "The siren howled, but I just sat there for a few seconds," he recalls. "A minute later the siren went off again. The second 40 missile was launched. Then the third and the fourth and the fifth."

CD 1-90

The system was telling him that the level of reliability of the alert was "highest." There could be little doubt. The Soviet Union was under attack. Petrov's duty in this case was clear. He was to pick up the phone that went straight to the nation's top military commanders and inform them of the 45 attack. It would be their job to order the counterstrike. As a soldier, obeying this order was the young officer's first <u>instinct</u>.

CD 1-91

But Petrov didn't obey. Something about the alert seemed strange. It was too strong and too clear. "There were 28 or 29 security levels. After the target was identified, the missiles had to pass all of those checkpoints. I was not 50 quite sure it was possible under those circumstances," he said.

CD 1-92

Petrov didn't pick up the phone to his commanding officers. Instead, he called a different number and reported a system <u>malfunction</u>. If he was wrong, the first nuclear explosions would hit the country minutes later. "23 minutes later I realized nothing had happened. If there had been a real 55 strike, then I would already know about it. It was such a relief."

CD 1-93

Petrov retired from the army with the rank of lieutenant colonel. He never received any praise for his actions, or lack of them, that night. Indeed, he himself did not mention the incident for 10 years, embarrassed that his country's security system had failed so badly. But after the collapse of the 60 Soviet Union, his story got into the newspapers, and he was given several international awards. But he still does not consider himself a hero. All he will say by way of self-congratulation was "they were lucky it was me on shift

UNIT 10 | An Ordinary Hero

that night."

1-94

Petrov's story serves as a powerful reminder of the impact that individuals, even those in relatively obscure positions, can have on the course of history. His courage and clear thinking in the face of overwhelming pressure demonstrate the strength of character required to make the right choice, regardless of personal risk. If the young officer had followed his orders that night, it is quite possible none of us would be here today. Sometimes all it takes to save the world is to be brave for five minutes.

65

70

NOTES

literal 文字通り   **nuclear Armageddon** 核のアルマゲドン   **struggle for supremacy** 覇権争い
capitalism 資本主義   **totalitarian** 全体主義   **brink of disaster** 災難の瀬戸際   **early
warning system** 早期警戒システム   **counterstrike** 反撃   **alert** 警報   **at stake** [ソビエト連邦
の存亡が] かかっていた   **howl** 鳴り響く   **lieutenant colonel** 中佐   **obscure position** 無名の
地位   **overwhelming** 圧倒的な

Reading Comprehension

Decide if each sentence is true or false.

1. [T / F]   Emerson's quotation suggests that only important people can become heroes.

2. [T / F]   The missile crisis in Cuba in 1962 almost led to a nuclear war between the United States and the Soviet Union.

3. [T / F]   The actions Petrov carried out went against the orders he had received.

4. [T / F]   Petrov reported a system malfunction instead of an actual missile attack.

5. [T / F]   Petrov received praise and recognition from the Soviet military for his actions.

Finding Details

Write down the answer to each question.

1. Where was a conflict indirectly involving the U.S. and the Soviet Union taking place in 1983?

_____

2. Why was it important for the Soviet military to detect American missiles before they hit?

_____

3. What does Petrov's story tell us about the impact individuals can have on historical events?

_____

Extend Your Vocabulary

Choose the correct word from the list to complete each sentence.

perseverance	quotation	catastrophe	instinct	malfunction

1. A _____ in the computer system stopped production at the factory.

2. We will need plenty of _____ if we are going to win the championship.

3. This _____ is taken from a famous book on philosophy.

4. The animal defended itself by _____ when it was attacked.

5. The oil spill caused an environmental _____.

Summary

Listen to the audio and fill in the spaces.

Even the most ordinary person can be a hero if they act (1) _____ at the right moment. Very few, however, can claim to achieve what Stanislav Petrov did in his moment of heroism: literally saving the world. A military officer in the Soviet Union during the Cold War, Petrov was (2) _____ the early warning systems for incoming missile attacks from the United States. Suddenly, on the night of September 26, 1983, the alarm sounded to signal an attack. Petrov's (3) _____ in this case was to call the nation's top commanders so they could order a counterstrike before the missiles hit. To do so, however, would almost certainly have started a nuclear war between the world's two (4) _____. Overcoming his panic, the young officer thought clearly and decided there was something not right about the alert. Perhaps it was just a malfunction in the system. His decision was correct, and on that day the world was saved from (5) _____ Armageddon.

Expressing Your Opinion

→ Discussion

What do you think about the following statement? Think of two reasons for your opinion and share them with your classmates. Try to add details or examples and continue your conversation for as long as you can.

The world should get rid of all its nuclear weapons.

5. Strongly Agree   4. Agree   3. Neither agree nor disagree

2. Disagree   1. Strongly disagree

Reason 1: _____

_____

_____

Reason 2: _____

_____

_____

→ Paragraph Writing

Finish this short paragraph about the opinion above. Give details or examples for your reasons.

I think / don't think that the world should get rid of all its nuclear weapons. First,

_____

_____

_____

_____

_____

_____

_____

UNIT 11

Left or Right

What is bias in the media?

Introduction

You might think that the newspapers you get delivered to your mailbox or the news shows you watch on television always provide reliable and accurate information. Unfortunately, the reality is more complicated than this. What is media bias and why is it important to know about it?

Activate Your Thinking

Think about the following questions and share your ideas with your classmates.

1. Do you read a newspaper or watch the news? What newspapers or shows do you like?

   _____

   _____

2. What are some recent news events you have been interested in?

   _____

   _____

Reading

 2-02~09

Read the passage and check that you understand the <u>underlined</u> words.

 2-02

Can you trust everything you read? When it comes to the internet, the answer is definitely no. Unless you are sure that the site is accurate and reliable, it is wise to take much of the information you find online with a large pinch of salt. But how about newspapers? Surely you can trust the information printed in the paper delivered to your mailbox each morning, can't you? After all, the articles are written by professional journalists whose work is fact-checked by an experienced team of editors. It's not likely they would include serious mistakes or misinformation.

 2-03

Or is it? Unfortunately, the issue of reliability in the media, be it national newspapers or television news, is not as straightforward as we might hope. Most media outlets are not neutral and disinterested distributors of facts. They are profit-driven corporations whose viewpoints often reflect those of the powerful people that own them. They may not make up stories that don't exist, as some disreputable internet sites do, but they do present and interpret events according to their own beliefs and <u>biases</u>, particularly when it comes to politics or international relations. Being aware of media bias is an important aspect of being a citizen in a democratic society.

 2-04

So, what is media bias and where does it come from? Broadly speaking, there are two strands of political beliefs, which are reflected in the media that reports on them: left-wing and right-wing. The two terms actually date from the French Revolution of 1789 when two groups of representatives emerged within the new French parliament. One group supported the king and the existing political system. They sat on the right side of the assembly hall. The other group, sitting on the left, wanted a republic and a new form of government. Since that time, politics has changed considerably; however, the distinction between left and right still continues.

 2-05

Left-wing political groups tend to emphasize social <u>equality</u>, liberal values, and government intervention in the economy. For example, they support a higher rate of taxation, particularly on the wealthier members of society, in order to fund national health and welfare systems. They emphasize the duty of the government to regulate companies into protecting the environment or respecting the rights of their workers. They are also more likely to push progressive causes such as sexual and racial equality.

2-06

On the other hand, right-wing groups often prioritize individual liberty, conservative values, and limited government involvement. They favor lower taxes to allow people to keep more of the money they earn. They argue that companies should be regulated only to a small degree so they are free to compete freely and pursue profit. And they tend to support policies that put traditional social values, like marriage and the family, ahead of more liberal ideals.

2-07

Modern political parties usually fall into one of the two camps, or somewhere in the middle. The same is true of media outlets. In the U.S. for example, the Republican Party of Donald Trump and George W. Bush is regarded as right-wing, while the Democratic Party of Joe Biden and Barack Obama leans more toward the left. In terms of the media, the cable news channel Fox News is on the right side of the political spectrum, as is the business newspaper *The Wall Street Journal*. *The New York Times*, meanwhile, is more left-wing, together with the news channel MSNBC. The two sides may report on the same political or international events but with very different interpretations. Here, for example, are two headlines from Fox News and MSNBC on the topic of President Biden's plan to invest money in infrastructure, such as bridges and roads:

"Biden's Radical Agenda: Massive Government Spending and Tax Hikes." (Fox News)

"Biden's Infrastructure Plan Aims to Rebuild America's Crumbling Infrastructure." (MSNBC)

2-08

The same bias can be seen in the media of other democratic countries, including Britain and Japan. In 2016, when Britain prepared to vote on whether to leave the European Union, the so-called "Brexit" referendum, the media was sharply divided between the two sides, with right-wing newspapers in favor of Brexit and left-wing papers against it. In that case, reporting went beyond differing interpretations of events and entered the realm of misinformation: spreading mistruths designed to influence the

perceptions of readers and society as a whole. It is hard to say exactly what
effect misinformation had on the Brexit vote – many factors were involved in
Britain's decision to leave the EU – but there is little doubt the media played
a significant role in pushing the vote one way or the other.

2-09

So, what can we do about media bias? Is it a problem that society has to
solve, or is it just a natural consequence of free speech, a principle vital to
the effective functioning of democracies? These are not easy questions to
answer. Ultimately, the power of the media comes down to individual
citizens and their ability to separate fact from opinion; that is, objective from
subjective reporting. When we open a newspaper or turn on the news, we
have to remember we are not seeing a completely neutral view of events.
Just as journalists interpret events in their own way, we have to do the same.

NOTES

take with a pinch of salt 完全には信じない，割り引いて聞く［直訳：一粒の塩を加えて食べる ⇒ 塩気の
ない物（＝信用できない話）はそのまま食べられない］　**misinformation** 誤報　**straightforward**
単純　**disinterested** 私欲のない，利害関係のない　**profit-driven** 利益を追求する，利益第一の
disreputable いかがわしい，評判の悪い　**strand** 系統　**parliament** 議会　**distinction** 区別
intervention in the economy 経済への介入　**progressive cause** 進歩的な大義　**liberty** 自由
pursue 追求する　**Republican Party** 共和党　**Democratic Party** 民主党　**tax hike** 増税
crumbling 崩れかけた　**referendum** 国民投票　**realm** 領域　**functioning** 機能（する）

Reading Comprehension

Decide if each sentence is true or false.

1. [T / F]　Newspaper articles are always reliable because they are fact-checked by editors.

2. [T / F]　In the French Revolution, representatives on the left side did not support the king.

3. [T / F]　A right-wing government is more likely to raise taxes.

4. [T / F]　In the "Brexit" referendum, the media shared the same interpretation of the issue.

5. [T / F]　It is hard to say whether society must solve the problem of media bias.

UNIT 11 | Left or Right

Finding Details

Write down the answer to each question.

1. What should you consider when evaluating information on the internet?

   _____

2. What are three key priorities of left-wing political groups?

   _____

3. What does the article suggest individuals should do when consuming news?

   _____

Extend Your Vocabulary

Choose the correct word from the list to complete each sentence.

bias	equality	interpretation	objective	subjective

1. It is just a _____ opinion, so you should make up your own mind about it.

2. The new law is designed to improve _____ between men and women.

3. Science should be _____ and based on clear evidence.

4. I didn't agree with the media's _____ of the event.

5. There is so much _____ in the media, I find it hard to know what's true.

77

Summary

Listen to the audio and fill in the spaces.

Most people are aware that the internet is not always the best place to find (1) _____ information. But how about newspapers and television news? While media corporations employ professional journalists and (2) _____, this does not mean reporting is objective and neutral. On the contrary, it is often biased toward one of the two strands of (3) _____ beliefs: left-wing and right-wing. While left-wing parties emphasize the role of government in social, economic, and (4) _____ affairs, right-wing parties push more for individual liberty and choice. When these beliefs are reflected in the media, they can lead to very different interpretations of the same events. It is hard to say whether media bias is a problem that has to be solved or not, but as citizens in a (5) _____ society, it is important to think critically about what we read and see.

UNIT 11 | Left or Right

Expressing Your Opinion

→ Discussion

What do you think about the following statement? Think of two reasons for your opinion and share them with your classmates. Try to add details or examples and continue your conversation for as long as you can.

Media bias is a problem society has to solve.

5. Strongly Agree   4. Agree   3. Neither agree nor disagree

2. Disagree   1. Strongly disagree

Reason 1: _____

_____

_____

Reason 2: _____

_____

_____

→ Paragraph Writing

Finish this short paragraph about the opinion above. Give details or examples for your reasons.

I think / don't think that media bias is a problem society has to solve. First, _____

_____

_____

_____

_____

_____

_____

_____

UNIT 12

Gaming to Success

Can video games be good for us?

Introduction

Go into an average home and you won't hear many parents telling their kids: "Don't forget to play more video games!" Gaming tends to be regarded as an unhealthy pastime, taking time away from more useful activities. But recent research is placing doubt on those views. Can video games actually help a child's development?

Activate Your Thinking

Think about the following questions and share your ideas with your classmates.

1. Do you like playing video games? What kinds of games do you play and how often?

   _____
   _____

2. Do you think video games are good for us or bad for us?

   _____
   _____

UNIT 12 | Gaming to Success

Reading

Read the passage and check that you understand the underlined words.

Video games are big business. In 2022, revenue in the industry exceeded well over $200 billion worldwide, with this figure set to increase significantly in the years to come. Games like *Mario*, *Call of Duty*, *FIFA*, and *Final Fantasy* have become cultural phenomena, with fans waiting for new installments with the kind of excitement once reserved for movie franchises like *Star Wars* or *The Matrix*. Video game streamers on YouTube or Twitch gather huge numbers of followers to watch them play, while esports players can earn millions competing in professional tournaments around the world. The Dota 2 tournament in 2021, known as The International 10, featured record prize money of $40 million.

Despite these incredible numbers, however, you don't get many parents encouraging their children to spend hours each day playing video games. Gaming tends to be seen as fundamentally unhealthy: a waste of time that would be better spent studying, hanging out with friends, or playing sports. There is also a danger of addiction, particularly among children and teenagers, a problem that is not only psychological but can be financial too. Many modern games offer in-game purchases for special equipment or outfits, and some players have been known to spend thousands of dollars a year feeding their desire for new items. Another issue is the possible link between gaming and aggression. Although there is little objective evidence proving that video games can lead to violent behavior in real life, many parents fear the effect on their children's brains from playing games that involve fighting, shooting, and killing.

So, is there any good news for worried moms and dads, save for the unlikely prospect of their child earning millions as a future esports star? Thankfully, it seems the answer is yes. There is a growing body of evidence that points not at the harm that can be caused by playing video games but the benefits. For instance, a recent study conducted at the University of Vermont in the U.S. examined cognitive data from 2,000 children between the ages of nine and 10, comparing those who played no games with those who played for three hours a day or more (an amount that exceeds official medical advice). The researchers had the participants carry out two tasks that tested their ability to control impulsive behavior and memorize information. They also measured the children's brain activity while doing so.

CD 2-15

35 The investigators found that the children who reported playing video games were faster and more accurate on both cognitive tasks. They were better at controlling their impulses and quicker at recalling information. Brain imaging showed higher activity in regions of the brain associated with attention and memory and lower activity in regions related to vision.

40 Researchers believe the latter might reflect a greater efficiency in visual processing, an aspect of cognitive activity fast-moving video games tend to demand.

CD 2-16

The Vermont project, known as the ABCD Study, is important because it uses a much larger sample size than is usual in this kind of research. In total,

45 12,000 children are involved, and their cognitive development will be tracked regularly as they grow into young adults. In terms of gaming, however, the research team is quick to point out that the findings do not prove a cause-and-effect relationship. It could be that children who are good at these kinds of cognitive tasks are naturally drawn to playing games. The

50 investigators also emphasize the study does not mean children should spend unlimited time on their computers or mobile devices. The negative consequences of excessive screen time, including social isolation and depression, cannot be ignored.

CD 2-17

Nevertheless, the evidence of cognitive effect is supported by other studies

55 that have been done on a smaller scale. A team from the University of Rochester, New York, had a group of individuals play action games for four days a week for a minimum of one hour a day, finding that they outperformed non-gamers at rapidly processing information, estimating numbers of objects, and switching between tasks. Another study from 2013

60 found that 50 hours of action gaming improved performance on a task commonly used to test pilots, focusing on their ability to manage multiple sources of information simultaneously. A third study investigated elderly people, discovering that video game play improved attention, memory, and mental flexibility, all things that tend to decline with age. Significantly, many

UNIT 12 | Gaming to Success

of these improvements persisted beyond the short term, suggesting gaming might even be used as a form of treatment to reduce the effects of aging.

2-18

So, what does this all tell us about the modern pastime of gaming? Bader Chaarani, the lead researcher of the ABCD Study, commented: "Many parents today are concerned about the effects of video games on their children's health and development, and as these games continue to proliferate among young people, it is crucial that we better understand both the positive and negative impact that such games may have." Like gaming itself, research into these matters is a relatively new development. There is still much we don't know about the effects on children's minds of not only gaming but modern technology in general. It is not easy being a parent nowadays, but hopefully science will soon be able to start providing some help.

NOTES

phenomena 現象［古代ギリシャ語のルーツのある **phenomenon** の複数形］　**installment** 新作，新エピソード　**reserved for** にしか許されない　**outfit** 衣装　**save for** 〜を除いて，〜以外　**prospect** 見込み　**cognitive** 認知的　**impulsive behavior** 衝動的行動　**drawn to** 引き付けられる，魅力を感じる　**excessive** 過度の　**outperform** 〜よりも優れている，を上回る　**simultaneously** 同時に　**persist** 持続する，とどまらない　**proliferate** 増える，増加する

Reading Comprehension

Decide if each sentence is true or false.

1. [T / F] Esports are still a relatively small business.

2. [T / F] It has not been proved that video games lead to violent behavior.

3. [T / F] Brain scans revealed no differences between gamers and non-gamers.

4. [T / F] A study showed you can improve mental performance by playing just 50 hours of action games.

5. [T / F] The researchers in the ABCD Study claim a cause-and-effect relationship between playing video games and cognitive improvements.

Finding Details

Write down the answer to each question.

1. Briefly, what is the second danger of video games mentioned in the second paragraph?

   _____

2. Why might gamers be more efficient at visual processing, according to the article?

   _____

3. Why is the Vermont study particularly important compared to other video game studies?

   _____

Extend Your Vocabulary

Choose the correct word from the list to complete each sentence.

exceed	addiction	purchase	recall	crucial

1. I cannot _____ what I was doing on that day.

2. The man decided to begin treatment for his alcohol _____.

3. I would like to return this recent _____ I made, as it doesn't seem to be working.

4. Recently, temperatures have begun to _____ 40 degrees in the summer.

5. It is absolutely _____ we find an answer to this problem.

84

UNIT 12 | Gaming to Success

Summary

 2-19

Listen to the audio and fill in the spaces.

Video gaming is a billion-dollar (1) _____ with huge rewards available for those good enough to do it professionally. But if you ask most parents, they won't express positive views. Video games are often seen, at best, as a (2) _____ of time and, at worst, as a potential route to addiction and even violence. A growing body of research, however, is pointing in the opposite direction, revealing games to be a source of cognitive (3) _____. A large-scale study at the University of Vermont, for example, found that children who played games for more than three hours a day performed better on tasks that tested their ability to control impulsive behavior and memorize information. They also appeared to be more (4) _____ at visual processing. Other studies have supported these findings, suggesting games might be used to improve mental (5) _____. Perhaps parents don't have to worry so much.

Expressing Your Opinion

→ Discussion

What do you think about the following statement? Think of two reasons for your opinion and share them with your classmates. Try to add details or examples and continue your conversation for as long as you can.

> It is good for children to play video games for a few hours each day.

5. Strongly Agree **4. Agree** **3. Neither agree nor disagree**
2. Disagree **1. Strongly disagree**

Reason 1: _____

_____

_____

Reason 2: _____

_____

_____

→ Paragraph Writing

Finish this short paragraph about the opinion above. Give details or examples for your reasons.

I think / don't think that it is good for children to play video games for a few

hours each day. First, _____

_____

_____

_____

_____

_____

86

UNIT 13

Digital Town Square

Why is Twitter always in the news?

Introduction

Twitter, or X as it is now called, is far from being the largest social media site in terms of users, and yet it seems to have more impact on daily events than any other. Political protests, natural disasters, and even wars often feature Twitter within their narratives. What is the secret of its influence, and is it good or bad?

Activate Your Thinking

Think about the following questions and share your ideas with your classmates.

1. Do you use Twitter (X) or other social media sites? How do you use them and for how long each day?

_____

_____

2. What are some good and bad points of social media in your opinion?

_____

_____

Reading

🎧 2-21〜27

Read the passage and check that you understand the underlined words.

🎧 2-21

When Elon Musk, CEO of Tesla Motors and SpaceX, announced his intention to buy Twitter (now known as X), he called the social media site a "digital town square." What he meant was that Twitter functions like the central square of an old city, where citizens would gather to share news, exchange opinions, and discuss the issues of the day. Twitter, Musk said, is "where matters vital to the future of humanity are debated." Since his $44 billion acquisition, however, it's fair to say things have not gone smoothly. Musk's cuts to the content moderation department, which was responsible for finding and removing harmful content, led to a large number of advertisers withdrawing their business out of fear their posts could appear side by side with hate speech or discrimination. Since advertising is the main source of income for the site, revenues took a significant hit. At the time of writing, the company is now worth just $15 billion, a third of the price Musk paid for it.

🎧 2-22

Twitter (or X) has approximately 380 million active users, which makes it only the 15th largest social network in the world, far behind bigger names like Facebook, YouTube, Instagram, TikTok, LinkedIn, and Weibo. It has also very rarely made a profit, its yearly income exceeding its costs only twice since its establishment in 2006. So, why does this comparatively small company seem to have such a large influence on daily events? Why is it always in the news?

🎧 2-23

To answer these questions, we first have to understand some of the advantages the site offers for its users. First and foremost, it serves as a convenient tool for communication and information dissemination. Its real-time nature allows people to share information and opinions instantly, making it a primary source for breaking news. This immediacy has played a pivotal role in various global events, including protests, natural disasters, and political movements. One example of this was the so-called Arab Spring of 2011 when Twitter was used by citizens of Egypt, Tunisia, Libya, and Bahrain to call for protests against their undemocratic governments. Some political commentators even called the uprisings the Twitter Revolution. Another

UNIT 13 | Digital Town Square

more recent example would be the war in Ukraine, where ordinary soldiers can relate scenes from the front lines, giving news organizations valuable sources of information that their own reporters are unable to access.

🎧 2-24

Twitter has also democratized communication to some extent, giving a voice to individuals and communities who may not have had a platform otherwise. Movements such as #BlackLivesMatter and #MeToo gained momentum through Twitter, demonstrating the site's capacity to start social justice conversations. Celebrities, artists, and politicians also make use of the site to give out information and updates. Artists can publicize their work while politicians are able to connect directly with voters, explaining their policies on public issues. During the 2016 U.S. presidential election, for instance, Donald Trump used Twitter to mobilize his supporters and bypass the mainstream news media.

🎧 2-25

This use of Twitter by powerful people like Trump highlighted, however, what many see as the dark side of the social media site. When news can be shared so quickly, it is hard to stop misleading or mistaken information spreading. In Trump's case, his refusal to accept the results of the 2020 election, when he was defeated by Joe Biden, led Twitter to eventually ban him from the site as he repeatedly called for his supporters to protest. Other examples of false stories include conspiracy theories about vaccines, COVID-19, climate change, and 5G technology, among other things. In fact, a study at MIT in 2018 found that false information spreads six times more quickly on Twitter than the truth, with fake stories being 70 percent more likely to be retweeted. Lies, unfortunately, are often more interesting than facts.

🎧 2-26

Another problem Twitter has is the amount of harassment and personal abuse that is sent through the site. The anonymous nature of many accounts allows people to write anything they like without consequences, and as a result content that is racist, sexist, or homophobic is a regular feature of Twitter discourse. Twitter's content moderation department has often struggled to remove harmful posts before they spread, and this problem has surely been worsened by Elon Musk's decision to reduce its workforce. His motivation for doing so, apart from a need to cut costs, was due to a third problem Twitter is often accused of: bias. Rightly or wrongly, tech companies like Twitter tend to be regarded as liberal or left-wing enterprises. Musk, and

89

others of the same opinion, believed that the site was deliberately favoring liberal causes over conservative ones, removing content of a right-wing nature while promoting more progressive views.

CD 2-27

Its former management always denied these accusations, but the fact they were made at all illustrates the tight line Twitter and other social media sites have to walk between content moderation and free speech. To what extent is Twitter responsible for the views people express on it? How does it distinguish between false stories and real ones? Does a "digital town square" mean any kind of opinion is permitted, however offensive? These questions are central to the information age, and whether you like it or not, Twitter is one of the places where the debate will take place.

NOTES

acquisition 買収　**content moderation** コンテンツ・モデレーション［インターネット上のコンテンツをチェックして，不適切なものを削除したりする仕事］　**comparatively** 比較的に　**instantly** すぐに　**breaking news** 最新ニュース，ニュース速報　**immediacy** 即時性　**pivotal** 極めて重要な　**political commentator** 政治評論家　**uprising** 暴動，反乱　**relate** 語る　**front lines** 前線　**democratize** 民主化する　**platform** プラットフォーム，舞台　**momentum** 勢い　**social justice** 社会正義　**mobilize** 動員する　**bypass** 迂回する　**misleading** 誤解を招く　**conspiracy theory** 陰謀説　**racist, sexist or homophobic** 人種差別的，性差別的，同性愛嫌悪的な　**discourse** 言説，談話　**enterprise** 事業　**deny an accusation** 告発を否定する，訴えを否認する　**illustrate** 例となる　**walk a tight line** 厳しい一線を歩く　**offensive** 不快な

Reading Comprehension

Decide if each sentence is true or false.

1. [T / F]　Elon Musk said Twitter should function like the central square of an old city.

2. [T / F]　Twitter is a profitable company.

3. [T / F]　Twitter allows the media to receive news it wouldn't usually be able to access.

4. [T / F]　Fake news tends to spread much more quickly on Twitter than the truth.

5. [T / F]　Twitter was accused by Musk of being biased in favor of conservative views.

UNIT 13 | Digital Town Square

Finding Details

Write down the answer to each question.

1. Why did revenues decline at Twitter after Musk made cuts to the content moderation department?

_____

2. Why was the Arab Spring of 2011 sometimes called the Twitter Revolution?

_____

3. What two social justice movements gained momentum through Twitter?

_____

Extend Your Vocabulary

Choose the correct word from the list to complete each sentence.

vital	withdraw	discrimination	protest	anonymous

1. I have to _____ some money from the cash machine.

2. It is _____ we work together to fight climate change.

3. Since the message was _____, nobody knew who had written it.

4. There is a big _____ planned in the city tonight so the roads are closed.

5. Too many people still face _____ in their everyday lives.

91

Summary

 2-28

Listen to the audio and fill in the spaces.

When Elon Musk decided to buy Twitter, he called it a "digital town square," referring to the old custom of (1) _____ in the central square of a city to discuss the important issues of the day. For a social media site with a comparatively small number of users, Twitter seems to have a surprisingly large (2) _____ on daily events. The ease with which people can share opinions and information makes it a convenient tool for disseminating breaking news, and this has given it a central (3) _____ in global events such as protests, political movements, and social justice campaigns. There is a dark side, however. Misinformation, harassment, and personal (4) _____ are also a feature of the site, with the company often unable to remove harmful content before it spreads. It walks a tight line between content moderation and free speech, a challenge (5) _____ by many social media companies today.

UNIT 13 | Digital Town Square

Expressing Your Opinion

→ Discussion

What do you think about the following statement? Think of two reasons for your opinion and share them with your classmates. Try to add details or examples and continue your conversation for as long as you can.

Twitter has a positive influence on the world.

5. Strongly Agree   **4. Agree**   **3. Neither agree nor disagree**
2. Disagree   **1. Strongly disagree**

Reason 1: _____

_____

_____

Reason 2: _____

_____

_____

→ Paragraph Writing

Finish this short paragraph about the opinion above. Give details or examples for your reasons.

I think / don't think that Twitter has a positive influence on the world. First, _____

_____

_____

_____

_____

_____

_____

93

UNIT 14

For Love Not Money

Is there a dark side to working in Hollywood?

Introduction

Working in Hollywood seems like a dream job. But in 2021 and again in 2023, thousands of workers within the television and movie business voted to go on strike, complaining of low salaries, insufficient break times, and unpaid overtime. Is there a dark side to working in the world's most glamorous industry?

Activate Your Thinking

Think about the following questions and share your ideas with your classmates.

1. Do you like watching Hollywood movies? What is your favorite movie?
   _____
   _____

2. Do you think you would enjoy working in the movie business? Why / why not?
   _____
   _____

UNIT 14 For Love Not Money

Reading

2-30〜37

Read the passage and check that you understand the underlined words.

2-30

Name a dream job, and working in Hollywood might be it. When we think of America's multibillion-dollar movie industry, we tend to imagine handsome actors and glamorous actresses, brilliant directors and powerful producers: highly paid artists who turn creative visions into feasts of entertainment for the big screen. Who hasn't watched the final credits of a hit movie and thought about what it must have been like to work toward its creation? For any aspiring actor, filmmaker, or screenwriter, Hollywood is the ultimate destination, the place where miracles happen and dreams come to life.

2-31

So, why in that case did 60,000 Hollywood film and television workers vote in October 2021 to go on strike for the first time in 128 years? Why did union leaders representing these workers describe their members as being "at breaking point" and "worried about how they're going to get their next meal on the table?" Is Hollywood not the dreamland we might imagine it to be?

2-32

The answer to that might depend on what you do there. While there are certainly great rewards, in terms of both riches and fame, to be had in Los Angeles's most famous district, there is also a culture of long hours, low pay, and perilous job security. The International Alliance of Theatrical Stage Employees (IATSE) represents almost all the professions that exist in the film industry behind the scenes, including set designers, artists, carpenters, makeup artists, animators, camera operators, sound technicians, and production assistants. It was they who held a vote on whether to strike for the first time in the union's history in protest at the working conditions of their members. Marisa Shipley, a regional director at IATSE, explained that many Hollywood workers get paid little more than the minimum wage of $15 an hour, a tiny amount for such an expensive part of the world. They are also expected to work excessive hours with irregular mealtimes and insufficient time off between shifts.

2-33

Noah Suarez-Sikes, a production assistant, is one of those suffering workers.

95

"There is an industry-wide problem of making people work overtime they're not paid for," he says. "You kind of accept this condition that you're going to do unpaid work; you can get called to work on weekends, you can be asked to do things late into the evening and outside of work hours."

CD 2-34

While behind-the-scenes workers have long been underpaid, the problem has worsened in recent years due to the coronavirus pandemic, which shut down virtually the entire industry. Many low-level employees chose to leave the film business, leaving fewer workers with an even greater workload when production resumed. Marisa Shipley says that movie studios are keeping people in low-paid entry positions much longer than in the past and, due to production pressures, forcing them to work longer hours. "It's absurd that an industry of billion-dollar corporations is not paying people wages to live on in Los Angeles," she complains.

CD 2-35

The proposed strike by the IATSE was publicly supported by some of Hollywood's biggest names, including directors Steven Spielberg and Christopher Nolan, and fortunately an agreement was reached before the strike was due to take place, improving working conditions and pay. But in 2023, another strike hit the industry, this time orchestrated by actors and writers. The issue in 2023 was not only low pay but also the threat posed to the livelihoods of creative workers by artificial intelligence. New generative AI programs like ChatGPT have the ability to produce long stretches of text from a single prompt, raising fears it could be used to produce entire film scripts for free. Movie studios would make the first draft of a script using AI and then hand it over to a professional writer for polishing and editing, paying this writer much less than the studios would have given for an original script. There is also a fear that AI could be used to replace "extras," or background actors, the people used in scenes behind the main characters. Movie executives apparently suggested they could pay background actors for a single day's work and then use their images in perpetuity.

CD 2-36

As in 2021, the dispute with actors and writers eventually ended with an agreement, as studios agreed to increase pay and limit the use of AI. However, it would be optimistic to imagine this will be the end of the issue. As the power of AI grows, it will become more and more tempting for studios to make use of it, particularly as profits within the industry are so hard to

UNIT 14 | For Love Not Money

come by. (Of all the TV streaming services, for example, only Netflix
regularly makes a profit.)

65

🎧 2-37

So, what does the future hold for the thousands of low-paid workers
struggling to make a living in Hollywood? Are things going to get better or
worse? This is hard to say, but it seems unlikely there will be great
improvements. Like illustrators within Japan's animation industry, who work
long hours for little pay, the rewards for most people within the movie
business are not financial. They work for love, not money. Ultimately,
however, everyone has to live, and if we want to continue enjoying top-
quality TV shows and movies, we have to make sure the people who make
them are properly compensated.

70

NOTES

glamorous 魅力的な，美しい　　**feast of entertainment** エンターテインメントの饗宴　　**aspiring**
~を目指す　　**perilous job security** 危険な雇用保障　　**behind the scenes** 舞台裏　　**carpenter**
大工　　**insufficient** 不十分な　　**virtually** 事実上，実質的には　　**absurd** ばかげている，不条理な
orchestrate 組織化する　　**pose a threat** ~を脅かす，脅威をもたらす　　**livelihood** 生活
generative AI 生成 AI　　**perpetuity** 永久に　　**compensate** 報酬を支払う

Reading Comprehension

Decide if each sentence is true or false.

1. [T / F]　　In 2021, Hollywood workers voted to strike for the first time in
over a century.

2. [T / F]　　It is common for Hollywood workers to work overtime without
pay.

3. [T / F]　　The coronavirus forced movie studios to pay their employees
higher salaries.

4. [T / F]　　It seems studios planned to use AI to replace background actors
in order to cut costs.

5. [T / F]　　Thanks to the deal made in 2023, creative workers have little to
fear from AI in the future.

Finding Details

Write down the answer to each question.

1. What is the name of the union that represents behind-the-scenes workers in film and television?

   _____

2. Why were there fewer Hollywood workers after the coronavirus pandemic?

   _____

3. Why might AI mean that writers get paid less for a movie script?

   _____

Extend Your Vocabulary

Choose the correct word from the list to complete each sentence.

union	profession	resume	dispute	tempting

1. The tennis match will _____ after the rain delay.

2. The company met with representatives from the _____ to make a deal.

3. It's a _____ offer but I'm afraid I have to say no.

4. Working in IT is a great _____ but you have to keep learning new skills.

5. There is a serious _____ about who owns the land.

UNIT 14 | For Love Not Money

Summary

 2-38

Listen to the audio and fill in the spaces.

Why did Hollywood workers (1) _____ to strike in 2021? You might think they have a dream job, working with the world's most famous stars to create movies for the big screen. But the reality for most behind-the-scenes employees is low pay, long hours, and little job security. In an attempt to (2) _____ better conditions, the IATSE union, which represents these workers, threatened a strike that would have shut down Hollywood's entire industry. Luckily, the movie studios offered them a (3) _____ before the strike took place, but two years later another dispute hit Hollywood, this time over the growing threat posed by artificial intelligence. Writers and actors feared they could be (4) _____ by computers that worked for free. This fight too ended in a (5) _____ for the little guys. However, in the long term, AI will surely bring changes to the world of entertainment.

Expressing Your Opinion

→ Discussion

What do you think about the following statement? Think of two reasons for your opinion and share them with your classmates. Try to add details or examples and continue your conversation for as long as you can.

Artificial intelligence will not be good for society.

5. Strongly Agree   4. Agree   3. Neither agree nor disagree
2. Disagree   1. Strongly disagree

Reason 1: _____

_____

_____

Reason 2: _____

_____

_____

→ Paragraph Writing

Finish this short paragraph about the opinion above. Give details or examples for your reasons.

I think / don't think that artificial intelligence will be good for society. First, _____

_____

_____

_____

_____

_____

_____

_____

100

UNIT 15

Entertainment Empire

How did Disney take over the world?

Introduction

In October 2023, The Walt Disney Company celebrated its 100th anniversary. It is now one of the most powerful entertainment empires in the world, but it all began with two young cartoonists in Kansas. How did Walt Disney and his friend Ubbe Iwerks fulfill their dreams?

Activate Your Thinking

Think about the following questions and share your ideas with your classmates.

1. Are you a fan of Disney? What characters or movies do you like?

   _____
   _____

2. Have you been to Tokyo Disneyland or Disneysea? What do you like or dislike about them?

   _____
   _____

101

> **Reading**

🎵 2-40~47

> **Read the passage and check that you understand the underlined words.**

🎵 2-40

On October 16, 2023, The Walt Disney Company celebrated its 100th anniversary. Worth around $150 billion and employing over 200,000 people, it is one of the most successful and influential media empires on the planet. But its journey was not always a smooth one. Disney has had both extraordinary successes and disastrous failures over its long history, as well as a number of controversies. How did it get to where it is today?

🎵 2-41

Let's start at the beginning. Walt Disney was born in Chicago in 1901, a keen cartoonist from a young age. He started his first animation company in Kansas at the age of 19 with his friend Ubbe Iwerks, but the business failed to get off the ground. Undeterred, the pair moved to Hollywood together with Walt's brother Roy, where they founded Walt Disney Studio. The fledgling company created animations for the much larger Universal Pictures, achieving early success with a character called Oswald the Lucky Rabbit. Unfortunately, a dispute with Universal in 1928 led them to lose the rights to Oswald, putting the company at the risk of failure. Luckily, Iwerks came up with another character almost immediately, one we're all familiar with today: Mickey Mouse. The first major release with Mickey, a short film called *Steamboat Willie*, which successfully synchronized sound and animation, was a massive hit, laying the foundation for everything Disney was to build.

🎵 2-42

Walt Disney himself, although a warm and friendly person in public, was shy and insecure in private. He was also very demanding of his staff. One former employee recalled that the highest praise you could ever get from the boss was: "That'll work." Through the creativity and work ethic of Walt and his team, Disney continued to push the boundaries of what was possible in animation, producing the first color cartoons and the first animated feature-length film, *Snow White and the Seven Dwarfs*. More films followed in *Bambi*, *Fantasia*, and *Cinderella*, regarded today as classics of the genre. The problem for Disney, however, was they were extremely expensive to make, requiring large revenues at the box office just to break even. One flop could

102

UNIT 15　Entertainment Empire

sink the studio.

🎧 2-43

Rather than play it safe, however, Walt decided to go bigger. He had long dreamed of creating a theme park to show off his growing cast of characters, and in 1955 he finally opened Disneyland in Anaheim, California, funding it, partly, using a loan from his own life insurance. Disneyland allowed Walt to pursue a "total merchandising" strategy, generating revenue not only from animations but also toys, food, clothes, accessories, and homeware. Still, it was not always smooth sailing. Walt's death in 1966 led to a creative hole at the top of the company and, despite the occasional success, many of its films failed to impress at the box office. The most reliable moneymakers were the theme parks. Walt Disney World opened in Florida in 1971 and Tokyo Disneyland followed 12 years later.

🎧 2-44

In terms of filmmaking, the turning point came with the selection of a new CEO, Michael Eisner, in 1984. As the public face of the organization, Eisner promoted the idea of a Disney Renaissance. Initially focusing on comedies and dramas for adults, Disney enjoyed a string of hits, including *Splash*, *The Color of Money*, and, on television, *The Golden Girls*. Successes with animations followed, with films like *Who Framed Roger Rabbit* and *The Little Mermaid*. In 1991, the musical *Beauty and the Beast* became the first animated film to be nominated for the Academy Award for Best Picture.

🎧 2-45

Since then, Disney's fortunes have continued to rise. Although Eisner eventually lost his position at the head of the company, his successor Bob Iger managed to maintain its winning run. Under his leadership, Disney acquired some of the most popular and profitable movie franchises of all time in Pixar, Marvel, and Star Wars, cementing its position at the very top of global entertainment.

🎧 2-46

As the Walt Disney Company enters its second century, however, the future is not clear. Disney's streaming service, Disney+, is deeply unprofitable, leading to rumors of substantial financial cuts as the company balances the need for a strong library of content with the exorbitant cost of creating new shows. There is criticism of the pay gap between top executives and ordinary workers, and there are persistent concerns about the degree of diversity within Disney's shows, both old and new. While the old cartoons tended to

reflect the differing morals of the time, modern productions have to be much
more open to minority voices and communities. This is a challenge Disney
65 has been active in taking on, and it must continue to be so in the future.

🎵 2-47

Despite the controversies, Disney is still an incredibly strong company,
generating income from many different areas. As it celebrates its 100th
birthday, it will surely be looking back to its humble beginnings: a young
70 boy called Walt scribbling cartoons in his bedroom and his good friend
Ubbe, who decided to draw a mouse.

NOTES

get off the ground 軌道に乗る   **undeterred** それでもめげずに   **fledgling** 駆け出しの，設立間も
ない   **synchronize** シンクロする   **lay the foundation** 基礎を築く   **insecure** 不安な，自信のな
い   **work ethic** 労働倫理   **feature-length** 長編   **at the box office** 興行的に［（映画館・劇場の）
チケット売り場］   **flop** 失敗   **smooth sailing** 順風満帆   **Academy Award** アカデミー賞
successor 後任   **cement** 固める   **substantial** 大幅な   **exorbitant** 法外な   **persistent** 根
強い   **minority voices** マイノリティの声   **humble** ささやかな，粗末な   **scribble** 落書きをする

Reading Comprehension

Decide if each sentence is true or false.

1. [T / F] Disney was founded by Walt Disney and his brother Roy in
Kansas.

2. [T / F] Walt Disney's private and public images were different.

3. [T / F] *Steamboat Willie* was Disney's first feature-length animation.

4. [T / F] Disney's animated films were known for being cost-effective to
produce.

5. [T / F] Both Michael Eisner and his successor brought success to Disney.

UNIT 15 | Entertainment Empire

Finding Details

Write down the answer to each question.

1. Why was Walt Disney Studio at the risk of failure in 1928?

_____

2. What was the key factor in Disney's "total merchandising" strategy?

_____

3. Why have there been rumors of cost-cutting at Disney in recent years?

_____

Extend Your Vocabulary

Choose the correct word from the list to complete each sentence.

controversy	rights	break even	acquire	diversity

1. The pop star was determined to keep the _____ to all her songs.

2. The _____ of the employees helps the company generate fresh ideas.

3. Unless we increase sales, we won't _____ this year.

4. I have been monitoring the reaction of social media to this latest _____.

5. The billionaire tried to _____ a popular soccer club in Spain.

Summary

 2-48

Listen to the audio and fill in the spaces.

As The Walt Disney Company (1) _____ its 100th anniversary, it's a good chance to look back at its history. How did a small animation company become such a powerful player in the world of entertainment? Walt Disney was born in 1901, moving to Hollywood as a young man to (2) _____ his dreams of becoming a cartoonist. The early years were hard, but when his friend Ubbe Iwerks (3) _____ the character of Mickey Mouse in 1928, the company began to take off. A key development was the establishment of the Disneyland theme park in California, which allowed the organization to expand its range of (4) _____. There were challenges, however. Following its (5) _____ death in 1966, Disney found it hard to produce hit movies. But the Disney Renaissance under new CEO Michael Eisner brought the good times back. Difficulties remain for the entertainment giant, but it appears determined to continue its success.

UNIT 15 | Entertainment Empire

Expressing Your Opinion

→ Discussion

What do you think about the following statement? Think of two reasons for your opinion and share them with your classmates. Try to add details or examples and continue your conversation for as long as you can.

> Disney will still be an important company in 50 years' time.

5. Strongly Agree   4. Agree   3. Neither agree nor disagree

2. Disagree   1. Strongly disagree

Reason 1: _____

_____

_____

Reason 2: _____

_____

_____

→ Paragraph Writing

Finish this short paragraph about the opinion above. Give details or examples for your reasons.

I think / don't think that Disney will still be an important company in 50 years'

time. First, _____

_____

_____

_____

_____

_____

_____

UNIT 16

Spooky Science

Are ghosts real?

Introduction

Surveys show that more than 50 percent of people in the United States believe in ghosts. A surprising number of people even claim to have seen one. But do ghosts really exist, or are they something invented by the human mind to explain spooky noises and sights?

Activate Your Thinking

Think about the following questions and share your ideas with your classmates.

1. Have you ever seen or heard a ghost?

_____

_____

2. Do you think that ghosts are real?

_____

_____

UNIT 16　Spooky Science

Reading

 2-50~57

Read the passage and check that you understand the underlined words.

2-50

William Johnson of Wisconsin in the United States was asleep in his bed when he was woken by a strange noise coming from the closet in his room. There was a scratching at the door, as if a cat or dog were attempting to get out. William's family didn't own a pet, so the 11-year-old knew it couldn't be an animal. As he opened his eyes and struggled to see in the darkness, the scratching grew louder. Fighting a rising sense of panic, the boy tried to turn on his bedside lamp. But, for some reason, his arm wouldn't obey him, refusing to move from his side. When he tried to scream out for his parents, he found he couldn't even do that. He was unable to speak or move.

2-51

The scratching grew louder and then suddenly there was a creak, like the slow opening of a door. A white figure appeared in the room, a young boy with a blurred face. The figure hovered in the air for a second and then disappeared, fading away into the darkness. William jumped in fright, his arm knocking the bedside lamp to the floor. The crash brought his parents running into the room. They turned on the light and saw their son sat up in bed, his face white with fear. The door of his closet was open.

2-52

William is a university student now, and to this day he still can't explain what he saw that night. Was it really a ghost, or was it just a dream or the overactive imagination of a young boy? For many people, the ghost explanation would not be so hard to believe. Surveys have shown that more than 50 percent of people in the United States believe in ghosts, and almost one in five say they have encountered a ghost themselves. There are popular TV shows in which so-called ghost hunters visit houses rumored to be haunted and try to pick up evidence of supernatural behavior through cameras and recording equipment.

2-53

But do ghosts exist, and, if not, what can explain the kind of experience William had? Scientists who have studied supernatural phenomena are quick to point out there is no evidence ghosts are real. Of all the ghost-hunting TV shows, not one has ever provided proof of ghosts. The explanation for

109

ghostly experiences, scientists say, lies not in the supernatural but in the equally mysterious human brain.

CD 2-54

Take, for example, William's feeling of not being able to speak or move. There is a scientific name for such a condition: sleep paralysis. Sleep paralysis happens when the brain messes up the process of falling asleep or waking. It is like "dreaming with your eyes open," says Baland Jalal, a neuroscientist at Harvard University. Dreaming usually occurs during a certain stage of sleep called rapid eye movement (REM), during which your eyes move around under their closed lids. Though your eyes move, the rest of your body can't, most likely to prevent you from acting out your dreams with your arms or legs. Your brain usually turns off this paralysis before you wake up, but in sleep paralysis you wake up while it's still happening. Sometimes it is accompanied by hallucinations, as your still-dreaming brain conjures up images that do not really exist.

CD 2-55

You don't have to experience sleep paralysis to see things that are not there. The human brain has to process a huge amount of information arriving through our eyes, ears, nose, and skin. It is impossible to pay attention to everything, so the brain picks out only the most important parts and fills in the rest itself. "The vast majority of perception is the brain filling in the gaps," explains David Smailes, a psychologist in the U.K.

CD 2-56

Most of the time, the picture created by the brain is accurate, but sometimes the brain adds things that aren't there. This phenomenon, known as pareidolia, is the reason we might look at the clouds and see shapes like rabbits, faces, or ships. The brain can also miss things that are there. A famous study in 1999 had people watch a video of basketball players passing a ball, asking participants to count the number of passes made. Halfway through the video, a man in a gorilla suit walks across the court. Asked whether they saw the gorilla, about half the participants said they missed it. They were in a state of absorption, so focused on their task they failed to see something right in front of their eyes.

CD 2-57

Studies have shown that some people are more prone to pareidolia and absorption than others. Likewise, some people are more likely to put their strange experiences down to ghosts. William himself is not one of them. He

UNIT 16 Spooky Science

believes the experience he had was probably his brain playing a trick on him. Perhaps he had sleep paralysis and a hallucination and perhaps he left the closet door open before he went to sleep. Scientists tend to agree with him. Before looking to the supernatural for explanations, they recommend we consider our own brains. They are just as interesting and mysterious as ghosts.

65

NOTES

scratching ひっかき音　　**creak** きしむ音　　**blurred** ぼやけた　　**hover in the air** 空中に浮かぶ
overactive imagination 過度の想像力　　**rumored** 噂されている　　**supernatural** 超自然的現象
mess up 台無しにする，間違える　　**neuroscientist** 神経科学者　　**conjure up** 想起させる
perception 知覚　　**prone to** 〜やすい，〜なりがち　　**absorption** 夢中になること　　**put ... down**
to 〜 …を〜のせいにする，〜と見なす

Reading Comprehension

Decide if each sentence is true or false.

1. [T / F] William thought an animal might be trying to escape from his closet.

2. [T / F] Ghost hunting shows have not managed to record figures that seem to be ghosts.

3. [T / F] Being unable to move is normal during the REM stage of sleep.

4. [T / F] Our perception of the world is based completely on our senses.

5. [T / F] The 1999 study was designed to study the phenomenon of pareidolia.

Finding Details

Write down the answer to each question.

1. What percentage of people in the U.S. say they have seen a ghost?

2. What phenomenon does Baland Jalal describe as being like "dreaming with your eyes open"?

3. What did half the participants in the 1999 study fail to notice?

Extend Your Vocabulary

Choose the correct word from the list to complete each sentence.

| fright | encounter | so-called | paralysis | hallucination |

1. The boy got a terrible _____ when he was woken by a loud noise.

2. Was it real or just an _____ ?

3. You don't know what you will _____ if you enter a haunted house.

4. Sleep _____ is like dreaming while you are awake.

5. Dreaming occurs during the _____ REM stage of sleep.

Summary

2-58

Listen to the audio and fill in the spaces.

When he was 11 years old, William had a very strange experience while asleep. After a scratching noise from his closet woke him up, he saw what looked like the (1) _____ of a young boy. Was it a ghost? A surprising number of people in the United States would believe so, but is there any (2) _____ ghosts are real? The answer is no. Scientists say ghosts are most likely tricks played on us by our brains. For example, a condition known as sleep paralysis can cause us to dream with our eyes open, (3) _____ hallucinations. It happens when our brains mess up the process of (4) _____ or waking up. There are also phenomena like pareidolia and absorption that can cause us to see things that aren't there or miss things that are. Scientists believe that supernatural mysteries can be explained by (5) _____ the human brain.

112

UNIT 16 | Spooky Science

Expressing Your Opinion

→ Discussion

What do you think about the following statement? Think of two reasons for your opinion and share them with your classmates. Try to add details or examples and continue your conversation for as long as you can.

It is strange to believe in ghosts.

5. Strongly Agree **4. Agree** **3. Neither agree nor disagree**
2. Disagree **1. Strongly disagree**

Reason 1: _____

_____

_____

Reason 2: _____

_____

_____

→ Paragraph Writing

Finish this short paragraph about the opinion above. Give details or examples for your reasons.

I think / don't think that it is strange to believe in ghosts. First, _____

_____

_____

_____

_____

_____

_____

_____

UNIT 17

Believing a Lie

Can we plant memories in the brain?

Introduction

Memories are a fundamental part of who we are as human beings. They influence our attitudes and shape our personalities. But not all memories are positive. Some can be extremely painful, even to the degree that they negatively impact our lives. Will we ever have the technology to delete unwanted memories or create new ones? And should we do so?

Activate Your Thinking

Think about the following questions and share your ideas with your classmates.

1. Do you have a good memory? Are you able to remember things easily?

_____

_____

2. What are your best or worst memories from your childhood?

_____

_____

114

Reading

Read the passage and check that you understand the underlined words.

The idea of implanting false memories into the human brain or erasing real ones has long been a theme of science fiction. In the film *Inception*, Leonardo DiCaprio's character places himself inside a man's dream with the aim of implanting an important idea into his subconscious. In *Eternal Sunshine of the Spotless Mind*, a couple whose relationship has ended painfully undergo a procedure to delete the memory of each other from their minds. In both movies, memory manipulation is treated as a feasible but unhealthy and potentially dangerous science. But how about in the real world? Is it possible to change people's memories and, if so, is it something we should ever do?

The first thing to note is that the process of forming and storing memories in the brain is extremely complex. The process by which information from our sensory experiences is transformed into mental images within the brain is known as "memory encoding," and it involves the strengthening of connections between neurons and the activation of specific neural circuits.

Once a memory is encoded, it must be stored for future retrieval. But this storage does not take place in one single part of the brain. The hippocampus, for example, is essential for turning short-term mental images, which might last for just 20 or 30 seconds, into long-term memories. It is the part of the brain we use when we actively try to remember something we have just seen or heard. Long-term memories are stored mostly in the cortex, the outer wrinkly part of our brain responsible for most of our conscious experience; however, they also remain partly in the hippocampus. Meanwhile, another part of the brain, the amygdala, is involved in the storage of strong emotions, like fear or pleasure. It organizes physical reactions to outside threats, such as the "fight or flight" response commonly seen in animals.

Although the field of memory research has come a long way in recent years, there are still many things not fully understood. As a result, we do not yet have the technology to implant or erase memories in the way science fiction movies have depicted. That said, there are elements of memory manipulation that have been achieved in either humans or animals. The first is the creation of false memories using techniques of suggestion. There have been many cases, both in psychological studies and in real life, of people being persuaded by skilled interviewers that fictitious events actually happened. In 1999, for example, researchers at the University of British Columbia managed to convince 26 percent of their subjects they had been victims of a vicious animal attack when they were children, even though no attack had taken place. This phenomenon of implanting false information is known as the "misinformation effect," and it is actually rather problematic. Criminal cases can often be decided by the testimony of eyewitnesses, who might be susceptible to suggestive questioning by lawyers or police.

🎧 2-64

In terms of more technological methods, scientists have succeeded in implanting artificial memories in mice using a technique called "optogenetics." Optogenetics allows researchers to control neurons within the brain by shining light on them. In a study published in 2014, a research team simultaneously activated an area of the brain related to the perception of odors and areas of the brain associated with either reward or aversion. They were able to make mice respond to an odor they had never smelled before as if they had. Another team achieved similar results by activating the brains of mice while they were asleep. In this study, memories of a particular location were implanted. When the mice woke up, they headed straight to that location and spent more time there than anywhere else.

🎧 2-65

Researchers have also been successful in erasing memories in mice. A team in the U.S. demonstrated that fearful memories of a sound associated with an electric shock could be turned off and on. The scientists were able to discover the specific brain cells where the memory was stored. By decreasing activity within those cells, they were able to delete the memory itself; by increasing activity, they could restore it. Professor Josselyn, the lead researcher, commented: "It really does give us proof of principle. If there's a memory problem, we don't have to target the entire body or the entire brain."

🎧 2-66

Erasing memories in humans has potentially important applications for the treatment of drug addiction or post-traumatic stress disorder (PTSD), a severe

UNIT 17 | Believing a Lie

mental illness caused by a reaction to an extremely stressful event. However, manipulating memories in mice is very different from doing so in human beings. First of all, our brains are far more complex, making it much more difficult to target where a particular memory is created or stored. Second, there are serious <u>ethical</u> considerations. Memories are a fundamental part of our personal identities. What would the effect be of erasing old memories or implanting false ones? As technology progresses, we seem to be getting closer and closer to the world of science fiction. In terms of memory implants, however, the future might still be a long way off.

65

70

NOTES

implant 植え付ける   **subconscious** 潜在意識   **undergo a procedure** 手術を受ける
memory manipulation 記憶操作   **feasible** 実現可能な   **sensory** 感覚的   **transform** 変換する   **memory encoding** 記憶の符号化   **neuron** ニューロン   **neural circuit** 神経回路
retrieval 検索   **hippocampus** 海馬   **wrinkly** しわくちゃな   **amygdala** 扁桃体   **fight or flight** 闘争か逃走か   **depict** 描く   **fictitious** 架空の   **vicious** 凶暴な   **testimony** 証言
susceptible to ～の影響を受けやすい   **optogenetics** 光遺伝学   **perception** 知覚   **odor** 匂い
aversion 嫌悪   **brain cell** 脳細胞

Reading Comprehension

Decide if each sentence is true or false.

1. [T / F]   Science fiction depicts memory manipulation as a safe and simple procedure.

2. [T / F]   Long-term memories are stored mainly in the hippocampus.

3. [T / F]   The "misinformation effect" involves convincing people that fictitious events happened.

4. [T / F]   In 2014, researchers successfully implanted the false memory of an odor in mice.

5. [T / F]   Doctors currently erase memories to help patients suffering from PTSD.

Finding Details

Write down the answer to each question.

1. Why did the couple in *Eternal Sunshine of the Spotless Mind* decide to have certain memories erased?

   _____

2. Which part of the brain is responsible for the "fight or flight" response in animals?

   _____

3. What memories did researchers in the U.S. erase in mice?

   _____

Extend Your Vocabulary

Choose the correct word from the list to complete each sentence.

erase	convince	eyewitness	application	ethical

1. Since the _____ was not reliable, the police could not be sure what happened.

2. I always back up my data in case I _____ it by mistake.

3. This is a serious _____ issue so science cannot help.

4. I managed to _____ my boss to give me some time off.

5. What will the first _____ of this technology be?

118

UNIT 17 Believing a Lie

Summary

 2-67

Listen to the audio and fill in the spaces.

Science fiction movies have often depicted a future in which human memories can be implanted or erased. But is this vision (1) _____? The answer is yes and no. On one hand, people's recollection of events can be manipulated through the power of (2) _____, a dangerous phenomenon when we consider how important eyewitnesses can be to solving crimes. In terms of implanting entirely new memories into the brain, however, this has only been done with mice. Using a technique called optogenetics, researchers (3) _____ implant memories of an odor that the mice had never smelled before. They were also able to erase (4) _____ memories by decreasing activity within particular brain cells. Mice brains, though, are much less complex than human brains, and there are (5) _____ and ethical reasons why we are still far from the world of science fiction.

Expressing Your Opinion

→ Discussion

What do you think about the following statement? Think of two reasons for your opinion and share them with your classmates. Try to add details or examples and continue your conversation for as long as you can.

It might be a good thing to manipulate or erase memories in a human being.

5. Strongly Agree   4. Agree   3. Neither agree nor disagree
2. Disagree   1. Strongly disagree

Reason 1: _____

_____

_____

Reason 2: _____

_____

_____

→ Paragraph Writing

Finish this short paragraph about the opinion above. Give details or examples for your reasons.

I think / don't think that it might be a good thing to manipulate or erase memories in a human being. First, _____

_____

_____

_____

_____

_____

UNIT 18

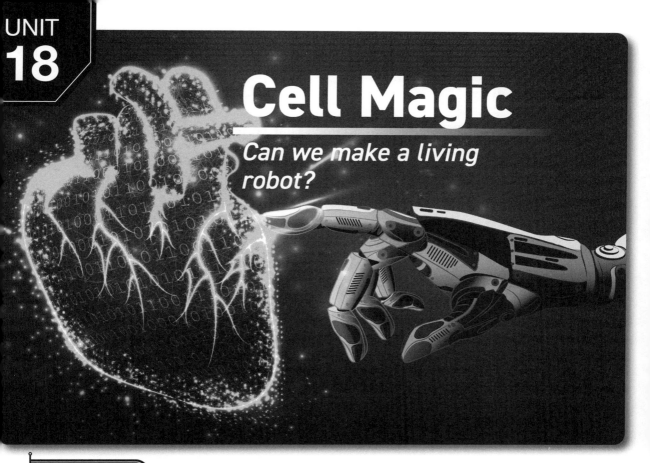

Cell Magic

Can we make a living robot?

Introduction

When we picture a robot, we usually imagine a metal machine carrying out a particular automated task. But some researchers are aiming to change that idea by creating robots out of the living cells of animals like frogs. These tiny machines are actually alive. What kind of work might they do?

Activate Your Thinking

Think about the following questions and share your ideas with your classmates.

1. What is your image of a robot? What kind of tasks do robots do now?

   _____
   _____

2. How do you think robots will develop from now on? What tasks might they do in the future?

   _____
   _____

Reading

Read the passage and check that you understand the underlined words.

When we think of the word robot, we tend to imagine electronic contraptions of metal and wires performing specific tasks like assembling cars in factories, collecting samples in space, or cleaning up dust in our homes. What generally doesn't come to mind is something that actually lives and breathes. Robots might be able to do more and more tasks once performed by manual labor, but they're not alive like humans, animals, or insects. They are machines, not organisms.

Science, however, looks set to change that idea. Some researchers are working on creating robots that blur the line between what is natural and what is artificial. Known as xenobots, a name almost as cool as the concept, these robots are synthetic lifeforms: living machines. The xenobots are created from cells, the microscopic building blocks that make up the bodies of all living creatures. Scientists extract cells from frog embryos and arrange them into structures so they can be programmed to move and carry out tasks: the definition of what a robot is.

The technology to create xenobots comes from a combination of biology and computer science. One of the major names in the fledgling science, Doug Blackiston of Tufts University in the U.S., got his inspiration for building them from a message he saw online from a group of scientists working with artificial intelligence. The team, based at the University of Vermont, was using AI to generate directions for making miniature robots that could perform a task. The robots were virtual not real, more of a concept than a reality, but Blackiston saw a challenge. He sent the Vermont team a message: "I bet I can build your models out of cells. A real-life version."

As a biologist, Blackiston had a lot of experience of working with stem cells, a special kind of cell that can develop into any type of tissue in the body. Extracting stem cells from frogs, he followed the plans produced by the Vermont team's computer program to shape the cells into various structures. He also added cells that would grow into heart tissue, predicting that once

UNIT 18 | Cell Magic

the tiny heart began to beat, the xenobot would have the ability to move on
its own.

🎧 2-73

The plan worked. Although not every design generated by the program
worked, some of the xenobots were able to move, change direction, and
push around objects: perform work, in other words, like a mechanical robot.
Amazingly, some even gained the ability to reproduce, a new form of
reproduction never seen in nature. The supercomputer came up with a
C-shape that resembled Pac-Man from the 1980s video game. The C-shaped
bot found hundreds of tiny stem cells in the petri dish and gathered them up
inside its mouth; a few days later the bundle of cells became new xenobots.
"I was astounded by it," said Michael Levin, a key member of Blackiston's
team. "Frogs have a way of reproducing that they normally use, but when
you liberate the cells from the rest of the embryo and you give them a
chance to figure out how to be in a new environment, not only do they
figure out a new way to move, but they also figure out apparently a new way
to reproduce."

🎧 2-74

The bots are extremely tiny, less than a millimeter wide. And since the
science is in the very early stages of development, there are no practical uses
for them yet. The potential applications, however, are varied and exciting.
One use could be in medicine, with the living robots programmed to deliver
drugs to exactly where they are needed inside the human body, the bots
harmlessly absorbed when they have completed their task. Another
application is environmental cleaning, such as collecting microplastics in the
ocean or removing pollutants from water. Since the xenobots are
biodegradable, they would not add to the pollution. A third use is simply the
study of life itself. If you are thinking about understanding how living
creatures work, biologists say, it makes sense to start with cells. The fact that
the frog stem cells invented an entirely new way to reproduce hints that
there are secrets to life still waiting to be discovered.

🎧 2-75

As with any new science, there are ethical considerations when it comes to
producing robots that are, in many ways, living organisms. Some critics
might argue that a robot that can reproduce itself is a frightening prospect.
What would happen if they somehow escaped into the real world? Could
they replicate themselves in sufficient numbers to pose a threat to the

environment? Doug Blackiston and his team acknowledge these concerns but stress that their work is strictly controlled and regulated. The xenobots are carefully contained in the laboratory and easily destroyed. The chances of them escaping and reproducing outside are extremely small.

CD 2-76

A living robot sounds like yet another idea from science fiction. While researchers like Blackiston and his team are still only just getting started, the day when there are synthetic organisms cleaning up pollution or delivering drugs inside our bodies may not be too far away.

NOTES

contraption 機械装置, 仕掛け   **blur the line** 境界線を曖昧にする   **synthetic lifeform** 人工生命体   **cell** 細胞   **microscopic** 微細な   **embryo** 胚   **fledgling** 駆け出しの   **stem cell** 幹細胞   **tissue** 組織   **resemble** 似る   **petri dish** ペトリ皿［発明者のドイツの細菌学者 Julius Petri （1852 ～ 1921 年） から］   **(be) astounded** 驚く   **liberate** 解放する   **pollutant** 汚染物質   **biodegradable** 生分解性   **prospect** 予感, 展望   **replicate themselves** 自己複製   **acknowledge** 認める

Reading Comprehension

Decide if each sentence is true or false.

1. [T / F]   The Vermont team had already created tiny robots that could move.

2. [T / F]   The xenobots were created with stem cells extracted from frog embryos.

3. [T / F]   Some xenobots came up with a new way to reproduce.

4. [T / F]   Although the technology is new, xenobots already have some practical uses.

5. [T / F]   Blackiston and his team have taken measures to prevent accidents with xenobots.

UNIT 18 | Cell Magic

Finding Details

Write down the answer to each question.

1. What two fields of science were combined to create living robots?

_____

2. Why wouldn't xenobots add to pollution in the environment?

_____

3. What ability shown by xenobots causes particular worry for critics?

_____

Extend Your Vocabulary

Choose the correct word from the list to complete each sentence.

assemble	organism	extract	reproduce	figure out

1. We need to _____ how this device works.

2. Since the instructions were not clear, it was hard to _____ the furniture.

3. This appears to be a new _____ never seen before in nature.

4. We have to be very careful when we _____ the cell from the sample.

5. All species must _____ to survive.

125

Summary

 2-77

Listen to the audio and fill in the spaces.

Robots can carry out more and more tasks that used to be done by human beings, but they are still machines, not living organisms. That, however, might be set to change. Doug Blackiston, a (1) _____ experienced with working with stem cells, has managed to create real living robots with the help of artificial intelligence. Blackiston extracted cells from frog embryos and shaped them into (2) _____ designed by a computer program. When he added heart cells, the tiny organisms were able to move, change direction, and push around objects: that is, (3) _____ work like a robot. The science is very new so there are no (4) _____ for the so-called xenobots yet. However, in the future, they could be used for delivering drugs in the human body, cleaning up (5) _____ , and uncovering new secrets to life. One day we may have to change our concept of what a robot is.

UNIT 18 | Cell Magic

Expressing Your Opinion

→ Discussion

What do you think about the following statement? Think of two reasons for your opinion and share them with your classmates. Try to add details or examples and continue your conversation for as long as you can.

> Robot technology will change the world in a positive way.

5. Strongly Agree   4. Agree   3. Neither agree nor disagree

2. Disagree   1. Strongly disagree

Reason 1: _____

_____

_____

Reason 2: _____

_____

_____

→ Paragraph Writing

Finish this short paragraph about the opinion above. Give details or examples for your reasons.

I think / don't think that robot technology will change the world in a positive

way. First, _____

_____

_____

_____

_____

_____

127

UNIT 19

Looking into the Past

What is the James Webb Space Telescope?

Jupiter taken by the James Webb Space Telescope

Introduction

In 2021, NASA carried out one of its most significant missions in decades: the launching of the James Webb Space Telescope. Delayed by 15 years, the launch took the telescope to a destination 1.5 million kilometers from Earth. What is special about the device, and why does it have to be so far away?

Activate Your Thinking

Think about the following questions and share your ideas with your classmates.

1. Are you interested in space? What kind of things interest you?

_____

_____

2. If you could, would you like to travel to space?

_____

_____

Reading

Read the passage and check that you understand the underlined words.

On Christmas Day, 2021, a very special rocket blasted off from the Guiana Space Center in French Guiana in South America. The rocket burned for 26 minutes to take it free of Earth's atmosphere and set it on course for a very specific area of our solar system. A spacecraft then separated from the rocket and flew for around a month, finally reaching its destination, around 1.5 million kilometers from Earth, on January 24. At that point, it deployed its very precious cargo: a telescope, the largest and most powerful ever sent to space. It was called the James Webb Space Telescope (JWST), named after one of NASA's early administrators, and it was designed to uncover the hidden secrets of our universe.

When we think of space telescopes, the first name that comes to mind is the Hubble, the still-active device that has been orbiting above Earth's atmosphere for more than three decades since its launch in 1990. The Hubble, taking advantage of the pure darkness of its environment, has captured some of the most iconic photographs of our universe ever taken: incredible pictures of distant galaxies, exploding stars, and awe-inspiring nebula. The James Webb telescope, however, while not replacing Hubble, is expected to bring images of even greater significance, ones that could change our entire understanding of the universe and its origins. Ones that, just maybe, might provide evidence of intelligent life in space.

To understand why, we have to consider the differences between Webb and Hubble. Fundamentally, Webb is not the same kind of optical device as Hubble and most Earth-based telescopes. It is not designed to capture visible light from space but infrared: light of much longer wavelengths. For most astronomical objects, infrared provides much more useful information than visible light. Unlike visible light, it is not blocked by dust and gas. It also provides data about the temperature of objects, giving astronomers a clue about what they are composed of. Finally, it is not affected by so-called "redshift," the phenomenon by which wavelengths lengthen due to the expansion of the universe, which causes distant galaxies to move further away from us.

🔊 2-82

Capturing infrared from Earth is very difficult since much of it is blocked by our planet's atmosphere. Moreover, Earth produces its own infrared emissions in the form of heat radiation, which tend to swamp the fainter astronomical sources. The best place for an infrared telescope, therefore, is out in space, as far as possible from Earth and all its unwanted sources of heat. At 1.5 million kilometers, the JWST is four times as far away as the Moon.

🔊 2-83

At this distance, Webb should be able to capture data that until now astronomers could only dream about. There are two main objectives for the telescope. One of its first tasks is a survey, called COSMOS-Webb, of the most distant galaxies in order to explore conditions at the dawn of the universe. JWST is sometimes called a time machine, because light traveling from huge distances takes so long to reach us that we are seeing objects not as they are in the present but how they were long in the past. NASA expects Webb to collect infrared data from around 13.6 billion years ago, soon after the universe itself began. By analyzing this information, scientists will be able to see how galaxies formed in the early universe and how they developed over time. They will also gain insights into the birth of stars, images that are hard to get with <u>conventional</u> telescopes because of the amount of space dust that tends to surround them. Visible light cannot penetrate through this dust but with infrared it becomes almost transparent.

🔊 2-84

The second major objective concerns the possibility of alien life. Astronomers have long been interested in the search for exoplanets, meaning planets that orbit around stars other than our own Sun. In particular, they want to find exoplanets that have the chemical ingredients and conditions necessary for supporting life: Earth-like planets, in other words, where life might have evolved just as it did here. JWST's ability to take incredibly high-resolution images should provide us with a direct view of planetary systems in their very earliest stages. It can examine the chemical composition of atmospheres, searching for signs they contain the building blocks of life. Who knows? Perhaps it will even find evidence of an extraterrestrial civilization.

UNIT 19 | Looking into the Past

2-85

NASA regards the construction and deployment of the Webb telescope as one of its greatest ever achievements. So complex and innovative was its design that it cost almost 20 times the original estimate of half a billion dollars and its launch was delayed by no fewer than 15 years. Its position so far from Earth means it cannot be maintained or fixed in the event of a fault. The enormous sunshield it carries, necessary for blocking the Sun's rays and keeping the telescope at a temperature of minus 233 degrees Celsius, had to be intricately folded up for transport and then opened up on arrival, with the slightest malfunction likely to make the device all but useless. NASA's success in deploying the telescope is hopefully only one of many triumphs to come.

NOTES

blast off 飛び立つ   **deploy** 配備する，展開する   **iconic** 有名な，象徴的な   **awe-inspiring** 敬の念を抱かせる   **nebula** 星雲   **infrared** 赤外線   **wavelength** 波長   **redshift** 赤方偏移 **swamp** 打ち消す   **faint** ほのかな，淡い   **insight** 洞察   **penetrate** 透過する   **exoplanet** 系外惑星   **planetary system** 惑星系   **extraterrestrial** 地球外   **intricately** 複雑に **malfunction** 故障

Reading Comprehension

Decide if each sentence is true or false.

1. [T / F]   The JWST is the first telescope sent up into space.

2. [T / F]   Infrared can help scientists to understand what a distant object is made of.

3. [T / F]   Heat from Earth means it is hard to pick up infrared emissions from deep space.

4. [T / F]   Ordinary telescopes cannot get clear images of stars as they are being formed.

5. [T / F]   Mars is an example of an exoplanet.

Finding Details

Write down the answer to each question.

1. What is the main difference between the JWST and the Hubble telescope?

_____

2. In what sense is the JWST like a time machine?

_____

3. Why does the JWST require a large sunshield?

_____

Extend Your Vocabulary

Choose the correct word from the list to complete each sentence.

orbit	distant	optical	composed of	conventional

1. We are still not sure what material the mysterious object is

_____.

2. On a clear night, you can sometimes see satellites as they

_____ Earth.

3. We need to throw away _____ thinking and come up with a new solution.

4. The trick art museum had many _____ illusions to entertain visitors.

5. It is hard to imagine how _____ stars are from Earth.

UNIT 19 | Looking into the Past

Summary

 2-86

Listen to the audio and fill in the spaces.

In 2021, NASA completed one of its greatest ever (1) _____: the successful deployment of the James Webb Space Telescope. Like the Hubble Telescope, which has been sending back incredible images of deep space for over 30 years, the JWST promises to revolutionize our understanding of the universe and its (2) _____. What makes the new telescope special is that it is designed to capture not visible light, which can be blocked by dust and gas, but infrared. Infrared will provide more data about the composition of (3) _____ objects and enable us to take pictures of the most distant galaxies. Because of the time it takes light from these galaxies to reach us, this means that the JWST will act as a kind of time machine, giving us a view of conditions at the (4) _____ of the universe. The telescope also aims to take images of Earth-like planets in other systems, providing the possibility of someday discovering an intelligent alien (5) _____.

Expressing Your Opinion

→ Discussion

What do you think about the following statement? Think of two reasons for your opinion and share them with your classmates. Try to add details or examples and continue your conversation for as long as you can.

One day we will find evidence of an intelligent alien civilization.

5. Strongly Agree   4. Agree   3. Neither agree nor disagree
2. Disagree   1. Strongly disagree

Reason 1: _____

_____

_____

Reason 2: _____

_____

_____

→ Paragraph Writing

Finish this short paragraph about the opinion above. Give details or examples for your reasons.

I think / don't think that one day we will find evidence of an intelligent alien civilization. First, _____

_____

_____

_____

_____

_____

_____

UNIT 20

A New Solution

Can we turn carbon dioxide into stone?

Introduction

The Hajar Mountains in Oman hold a secret. Originating from deep within the mantle far below Earth's surface, the mountains are made of rocks with a natural capacity to absorb carbon dioxide. Could they be the key to solving the world's most important environmental problem?

Activate Your Thinking

Think about the following questions and share your ideas with your classmates.

1. Are you interested in environmental issues? What issues do you think are most important?

   _____

   _____

2. How do you think we should solve the problem of global warming?

   _____

   _____

135

Reading

Read the passage and check that you understand the underlined words.

In northeastern Oman in the Middle East, a spectacular range of mountains rises up above the desert. The Hajar Mountains attract adventurous tourists from all over the world, but there are some visitors who travel to the remote location not for the dramatic views but for a secret hidden within the very rocks the mountains are made of. For geologists Peter Kelemen and his collaborator Juerg Matter, the Hajar Mountains could hold the key to solving the world's most pressing environmental problem: global warming.

As most people are aware, the major cause of global warming is the build-up of carbon dioxide in the atmosphere, which traps heat and prevents it leaving Earth. Carbon dioxide emissions have risen dramatically over the last century and continue to be extremely high today, reaching over 37 billion tons in 2022. As well as trying to cut our emissions – the only practical long-term solution – scientists are also exploring ways of removing existing CO_2 from the atmosphere in an attempt to limit the rise in temperatures before it is too late. One issue, however, is where to safely store the gas once it is removed, particularly considering the massive amount we are talking about.

This is where the Hajar Mountains come in. A large area within the range is composed of rocks that come directly from the mantle, the middle layer of our planet that starts about 10 kilometers below the ground. These rocks contain high levels of calcium and magnesium silicates, unusual minerals that naturally absorb CO_2 from the air. When rain falls, carbon dioxide within the water attaches to the silicate atoms in the rocks, forming a solid white mineral that traps the greenhouse gas. Kelemen estimates the mountains are naturally absorbing 50,000 to 100,000 tons of carbon dioxide per year. While this is a small amount in the context of global emissions, the geologist believes the rocks could one day solidify up to a billion tons each year. Other rock formations around the world, including in Iceland, could capture another 10 to 20 billion tons. "You're looking at something that could potentially have an impact on the human global carbon budget," he says.

UNIT 20 | **A New Solution**

CD 2-91

The key to making silicate rocks a practical measure against global warming is increasing the speed of carbon absorption. In Iceland, a company called Carbfix is conducting real-world experiments to dispose of carbon dioxide released by a geothermal power plant taking energy from one of the country's many volcanoes. Carbfix drilled a hole 400 meters underground and pumped in water containing high levels of CO_2. Tests revealed that as the water seeped into the rocks beneath the hole, the carbon began to disappear. Within two years, over 95 percent of the CO_2 had been absorbed, forming solid white veins within the rock.

CD 2-92

The Iceland project is now solidifying 10,000 tons of carbon dioxide per year, the first step before hopefully expanding the process to other parts of the country. In the Hajar Mountains, similar experiments are being conducted. With the help of Keleman and Matter, an Omani company is aiming to remove a billion tons of carbon dioxide a year by pressurizing it into water and injecting it three kilometers underground. The high heat and pressure at that depth should speed up the chemical reactions that turn CO_2 into stone, allowing more and more to be pumped in at greater speeds. As in Iceland, the work is still at a testing stage since drilling holes so deep is a challenging endeavor. "This test is just to demonstrate that the reaction is fast enough," Matter says.

CD 2-93

Unfortunately, the long-term success of the project depends not only on scientific results. Before CO_2 can be injected underground, it has to be captured from the air, and the technology to do that is not cheap. Although the cost is likely to come down over time, it will require a significant investment from governments. At present, gathering a billion tons of CO_2 from the air would require thousands of machines, each the size of a truck. Together, they would use as much electricity as a small country. This electricity would obviously have to come from renewable sources like solar power in order to stop yet more carbon dioxide being released into the atmosphere.

CD 2-94

The good news is that the one thing Oman has plenty of is sunshine. Some 600 square kilometers of solar panels would supply the electricity needed. As Ajay Gambhir, an economist at Imperial College London, notes, "It's not insurmountable. But it's a bit of a challenge." To remove 20 billion tons of

CO_2, the kind of amount necessary to provide a real solution to global warming, 20 of these massive operations would be required, or hundreds of smaller ones.

2-95

Keleman and Matter are aware of the difficulties, judging that the technology is at least 20 years away from being practical. But starting work on such projects now is the right thing to do. Global warming is not an issue we can wait to fix.

65

70

NOTES

remote 人里離れた　　**geologist** 地質学者　　**pressing** 差し迫った　　**calcium and magnesium silicate** カルシウムとケイ酸マグネシウム　　**mineral** 鉱物　　**solidify** 固める　　**capture** 捕獲する **carbon budget** 炭素収支　　**dispose of** 処理する　　**geothermal power plant** 地熱発電所 **seep** 染み込む　　**white vein** 白い鉱脈　　**pressurize** 加圧する　　**endeavor** 作業　　**not insurmountable** 乗り越えられないことはない

Reading Comprehension

Decide if each sentence is true or false.

1. [T / F]　The best long-term solution for global warming is to remove CO_2 from the atmosphere.

2. [T / F]　The Hajar Mountains are already absorbing CO_2 without using technology.

3. [T / F]　The test in Iceland did not appear to be successful.

4. [T / F]　Carbon capture machines require a lot of electric power.

5. [T / F]　Keleman and Matter believe it may be two decades before the technology can be used on a large enough scale.

UNIT 20 | A New Solution

Finding Details

Write down the answer to each question.

1. What part of Earth do the rocks in the Hajar Mountains come from?

_____

2. What is the advantage of injecting the water three kilometers underground?

_____

3. Why is cooperation from governments required to make the Omani project a real success?

_____

Extend Your Vocabulary

Choose the correct word from the list to complete each sentence.

emissions	amount	absorb	inject	economist

1. The news show interviewed a well-known _____ to explain the issue.

2. This stew requires only a small _____ of salt and pepper.

3. Researchers showed that _____ from the factory were causing health problems.

4. We plan to _____ the new gene into the organism.

5. Watch how quickly this new sponge can _____ the liquid.

139

Summary

 2-96

Listen to the audio and fill in the spaces.

Most people agree that global warming is the largest (1) _____ challenge faced by the world today. In the long term, the only real solution to the problem is to dramatically reduce our emissions of carbon dioxide. But scientists are also looking for ways to remove CO_2 from the (2) _____ and store it safely. One surprising way to do that has been found in the Hajar Mountains in Oman. The rocks from which the mountains are (3) _____ come from deep within the mantle and they contain high levels of a mineral that naturally absorbs CO_2 and solidifies it into stone. Geologist Peter Kelemen believes that if the (4) _____ can be speeded up, rock formations around the world could absorb up to 20 billion tons of carbon dioxide a year. There are significant challenges of cost and scale, but one day it could become a (5) _____ solution to Earth's most important problem.

UNIT 20 | A New Solution

Expressing Your Opinion

→ Discussion

What do you think about the following statement? Think of two reasons for your opinion and share them with your classmates. Try to add details or examples and continue your conversation for as long as you can.

Human beings will solve the problem of global warming before it is too late.

5. Strongly Agree   4. Agree   3. Neither agree nor disagree

2. Disagree   1. Strongly disagree

Reason 1: _____

_____

_____

Reason 2: _____

_____

_____

→ Paragraph Writing

Finish this short paragraph about the opinion above. Give details or examples for your reasons.

I think / don't think that human beings will solve the problem of global warming before it is too late. First, _____

_____

_____

_____

_____

_____

_____

Key Vocabulary

A

absorb (vb.)
accommodation (n.)
accomplish (vb.)
acquire (vb.)
addiction (n.)
amount (n.)
annual (adj.)
anonymous (adj.)
anxiety (n.)
application (n.)
assemble (vb.)

B

bias (n.)
break even (vb.)

C

catastrophe (n.)
civilization (n.)
collaborate (vb.)
composed of (vb.)
congestion (n.)
conserve (vb.)
context (n.)
controversy (n.)
conventional (adj.)
convince (vb.)
courageous (adj.)
crucial (adj.)

D

define (vb.)
discrimination (n.)
dispute (n. / vb.)
distant (adj.)
diversity (n.)

E

economist (n.)
ecosystem (n.)
effective (adj.)
eliminate (vb.)
emissions (n.)
encounter (n. / vb.)
ensure (vb.)
equality (n.)
erase (vb.)
ethical (adj.)
evolve (vb.)
exaggerate (vb.)
exceed (vb.)
executive (n.)
exhausting (adj.)
expedition (n.)
extract (n. / vb.)
eyewitness (n.)

F

figure out (vb.)
foster (vb.)
fright (n.)
fundamental (adj.)

H

hallucination (n.)
hesitate (vb.)

I

implement (vb.)
inject (vb.)
instinct (n.)
interaction (n.)
interpretation (n.)
invest (vb.)

M

malfunction (n.)
manufacture (vb.)
monitor (vb.)

O

objective (adj.)
optical (adj.)
orbit (n. / vb.)
organism (n.)

P

paralysis (n.)
participant (n.)
perseverence (n.)
phenomenon (n.)
priority (n.)
productivity (n.)
profession (n.)
protest (n./ vb.)
publicity (n.)
purchase (n. / vb.)

Q

quotation (n.)

R

recall (vb.)

recognize (vb.)

regret (n. / vb.)

reproduce (vb.)

resume (vb.)

revenue (n.)

right(s) (n.)

rural (adj.)

S

sample (n.)

so-called (adj.)

species (n.)

straightaway (adj.)

subject (n.)

subjective (adj.)

suburbs (n.)

survey (n.)

suspicion (n.)

T

tempting (adj.)

trace (n.)

U

union (n.)

V

valuable (adj.)

vital (adj.)

W

withdraw (vb.)

TEXT PRODUCTION STAFF

edited by	編集
Minako Hagiwara	萩原 美奈子

cover design by	表紙デザイン
Nobuyoshi Fujino	藤野 伸芳

CD PRODUCTION STAFF

narrated by	吹き込み者
Jennifer Okano （AmE）	ジェニファー・オカノ（アメリカ英語）

Our World, Our Stories
変動する世界と現代社会の再発見

2025年1月20日　初版発行
2025年2月15日　第2刷発行

著　者　Dave Rear

発 行 者　佐野 英一郎

発 行 所　株式会社 成 美 堂
　　　　　〒101-0052　東京都千代田区神田小川町3-22
　　　　　TEL 03-3291-2261　FAX 03-3293-5490
　　　　　https://www.seibido.co.jp

印刷・製本　萩原印刷株式会社

ISBN 978-4-7919-7317-0　　　　　　　　Printed in Japan

・落丁・乱丁本はお取り替えします。
・本書の無断複写は、著作権上の例外を除き著作権侵害となります。